What People Are [barcode] Threshold Bible Study

"Besides furnishing the reader with solid biblical analysis, this remarkable series provides a method of study and reflection, for both individuals and groups, that is bound to produce rich fruit. This well developed thematic approach to Bible study is meant to wed serious study and personal prayer within a reflective context. Stephen Binz is to be applauded for this fine addition to Bible study programs."
Dianne Bergant, C.S.A.
Professor of Old Testament
Catholic Theological Union, Chicago

"Threshold Bible Study is a wonderful series that helps modern people read the Bible with insight and joy. Each book highlights an important theme and helps us hear and respond to God speaking to us in the Scriptures. "
Richard J. Clifford, S.J.
Professor of Biblical Studies
Weston Jesuit School of Theology, Cambridge, Massachusetts

"Stephen Binz's Threshold Bible Study is a marvelous project. With lucidity and creativity, Binz offers today's believing communities a rich and accessible treasury of biblical scholarship. The series' brilliance lies in its simplicity of presentation complemented by critical depth of thought and reflective insight. This is a wonderful gift for personal and communal study, especially for those wishing to make a home for the word in their hearts."
Carol J. Dempsey, OP, Associate Professor of Theology, University of Portland, Oregon

"Threshold Bible Study accurately describes this user-friendly series that is aimed at anyone interested in a serious study of the Bible whether alone or in a group. Written in a sprightly easy-to-understand style, these volumes will engage the mind, heart, and spirit of the reader who utilizes the helpful resources author Stephen J. Binz makes available."
Alexander A. Di Lella, O.F.M.
Andrews-Kelly-Ryan Professor of Biblical Studies
The Catholic University of America

"Threshold Bible Study successfully bridges the painful gap between solid biblical scholarship and the rich spiritual nourishment that we expect to find in the words of Scripture. In this way, indispensable biblical knowledge leads to that spiritual wisdom which enables us to live in accord with God's purposes. Stephen Binz is to be congratulated for responding to this urgent need in today's world."
Demetrius Dumm, O.S.B.
Professor of New Testament, Saint Vincent Seminary
Saint Vincent Archabbey, Latrobe, Pennsylvania

"Threshold Bible Study offers a marvelous new approach for individuals and groups to study themes in our rich biblical and theological tradition. Moving through these thematic units feels like gazing at panels of stained glass windows, viewing similar images through different lights."
John Endres, S.J., Professor of Scripture
Jesuit School of Theology, Berkeley

"Stephen Binz has an amazing gift for making the meaning of the biblical text come alive! With a strong background in Bible study, he knows how to provide the roadmap any group can use to explore Scripture. Using the method known as *lectio divina*, Threshold Bible Study provides two things: growth in understanding the sacred text, and at the same time, the opportunity for actual conversion as the text is broken open and shared. I'd like to see this in the hands of every adult Catholic in the church today."
Bill Huebsch, theologian, speaker, and author of *Growing Faith Project*

"Threshold Bible Study is a refreshing approach to enable participants to ponder the Scriptures more deeply. The thematic material is clearly presented with a mix of information and spiritual nourishment. The questions are thoughtful and the principles for group discussion are quite helpful. This series provides a practical way for faithful people to get to know the Bible better and to enjoy the fruits of biblical prayer."
Irene Nowell, O.S.B., Mount St. Scholastica, Atchison, Kansas

"Threshold Bible Study is appropriately named, for its commentary and study questions bring people to the threshold of the text and invite them in. The questions guide but do not dominate. They lead readers to ponder and wrestle with the biblical passages and take them across the threshold toward life with God. Stephen Binz's work stands in the tradition of the biblical renewal movement and brings it back to life. We need more of this in the church."
Kathleen M. O'Connor, Professor of Old Testament
Columbia Theological Seminary

"I most strongly recommend Stephen Binz's Threshold Bible Study for adult Bible classes, religious education, and personal spiritual enrichment. The series is exceptional for its scholarly solidity, pastoral practicality, and clarity of presentation. The church owes Binz a great debt of gratitude for his generous and competent labor in the service of the word of God."
Peter C. Phan, The Ignacio Ellacuria Professor of Catholic Social Thought
Georgetown University

"Threshold Bible Study unlocks the Scriptures and ushers the reader over the threshold into the world of God's living word. The world of the Bible comes alive with new meaning and understanding for our times. This series enables the reader to appreciate contemporary biblical scholarship and the meaning of God's word. This is the best material I have seen for serious Bible study."
Most Reverend Donald W. Trautman, Bishop of Erie

Stewardship
of the Earth

Stephen J. Binz

TWENTY
THIRD *23rd*
PUBLICATIONS

Twenty-Third Publications
A Division of Bayard
One Montauk Avenue, Suite 200
New London, CT 06320
(860)437-3012 or (800) 321-0411
www.23rdpublications.com

ISBN 978-1-58595-373-8
Library of Congress Catalog Card Number: 2006937354
Printed in the U.S.A.

Contents

LESSONS 13–18

LESSONS 19–24

LESSONS 25–30

How to Use
Threshold Bible Study

Each book in the Threshold Bible Study series is designed to lead you through a new doorway of biblical awareness, to accompany you across a unique threshold of understanding. The characters, places, and images that you encounter in each of these topical studies will help you explore fresh dimensions of your faith and discover richer insights for your spiritual life.

Threshold Bible Study covers biblical themes in depth in a short amount of time. Unlike more traditional Bible studies that treat a biblical book or series of books, Threshold Bible Study aims to address specific topics within the entire Bible. The goal is not for you to comprehend everything about each passage, but rather for you to understand what a variety of passages from different books of the Bible reveals about the topic of each study.

Threshold Bible Study offers you an opportunity to explore the entire Bible from the viewpoint of a variety of different themes. The commentary that follows each biblical passage launches your reflection about that passage and helps you begin to see its significance within the context of your contemporary experience. The questions following the commentary challenge you to understand the passage more fully and apply it to your own life. The prayer starter helps conclude your study by integrating learning into your relationship with God.

These studies are designed for maximum flexibility. Each study is presented in a workbook format, with sections for reading, reflecting, writing, discussing, and praying. Space for writing after each question is ideal for personal study and allows group members to prepare in advance for their discussion. The thirty lessons in each topic may be used by an individual over the period of a month, or by a group for six sessions, with lessons to be studied each week before the next group meeting. These studies are ideal for Bible study groups, small Christian communities, adult faith formation, student groups, Sunday school, neighborhood groups, and family reading, as well as for individual learning.

The method of Threshold Bible Study is rooted in the classical tradition of *lectio divina*, an ancient yet contemporary means for reading the Scriptures reflectively and prayerfully. Reading and interpreting the text (*lectio*) is followed by reflective meditation on its message (*meditatio*). This reading and reflecting flows into prayer from the heart (*oratio* and *contemplatio*).

This ancient method assures us that Bible study is a matter of both the mind and the heart. It is not just an intellectual exercise to learn more and be able to discuss the Bible with others. It is, more importantly, a transforming experience. Reflecting on God's word, guided by the Holy Spirit, illumines the mind with wisdom and stirs the heart with zeal.

Following the personal Bible study, Threshold Bible Study offers a method for extending *lectio divina* into a weekly conversation with a small group. This communal experience will allow participants to enhance their appreciation of the message and build up a spiritual community (*collatio*). The end result will be to increase not only individual faith, but also faithful witness in the context of daily life (*operatio*).

Through the spiritual disciplines of Scripture reading, study, reflection, conversation, and prayer, you will experience God's grace more abundantly as your life is rooted more deeply in Christ. The risen Jesus said: "Listen! I am standing at the door, knocking; if you hear my voice and open the door, I will come in to you and eat with you, and you with me" (Rev 3:20). Listen to the word of God, open the door, and cross the threshold to an unimaginable dwelling with God!

SUGGESTIONS FOR INDIVIDUAL STUDY

• Make your Bible reading a time of prayer. Ask for God's guidance as your read the Scriptures.

• Try to study daily, or as often as possible according to the circumstances of your life.

• Read the Bible passage carefully, trying to understand both its meaning and its personal application as you read. Some persons find it helpful to read the passage aloud.

• Read the passage in another Bible translation. Each version adds to your understanding of the original text.

• Allow the commentary to help you comprehend and apply the scriptural text. The commentary is only a beginning, not the last word on the meaning of the passage.

• After reflecting on each question, write out your responses. The very act of writing will help you clarify your thoughts, bring new insights, and amplify your understanding.

• As you reflect on your answers, think about how you can live God's word in the context of your daily life.

• Conclude each daily lesson by reading the prayer and continuing with your own prayer from the heart.

• Make sure your reflections and prayers are matters of both the mind and the heart. A true encounter with God's word is always a transforming experience.

• Choose a word or a phrase from the lesson to carry with you throughout the day as a reminder of your encounter with God's life-changing word.

• Share your learning experience with at least one other person whom you trust for additional insights and affirmation. The ideal way to share learning is in a small group that meets regularly.

SUGGESTIONS FOR GROUP STUDY

• Meet regularly; weekly is ideal. Try to be on time and make attendance a high priority for the sake of the group. The average group meets for about an hour.

• Open each session with a prepared prayer, a song, or a reflection. Find some appropriate way to bring the group from the workaday world into a sacred time of graced sharing.

• If you have not been together before, nametags are very helpful as a group begins to become acquainted with the other group members.

• Spend the first session getting acquainted with one another, reading the Introduction aloud and discussing the questions that follow.

• Appoint a group facilitator to provide guidance to the discussion. The role of facilitator may rotate among members each week. The facilitator simply keeps the discussion on track; each person shares responsibility for the group. There is no need for the facilitator to be a trained teacher.

• Try to study the six lessons on your own during the week. When you have done your own reflection and written your own answers, you will be better prepared to discuss the six scriptural lessons with the group. If you have not had an opportunity to study the passages during the week, meet with the group anyway to share support and insights.

• Participate in the discussion as much as you are able, offering your thoughts, insights, feelings, and decisions. You learn by sharing with others the fruits of your study.

• Be careful not to dominate the discussion. It is important that everyone in the group be offered an equal opportunity to share the results of their work. Try to link what you say to the comments of others so that the group remains on the topic.

• When discussing your own personal thoughts or feelings, use "I" language. Be as personal and honest as appropriate and be very cautious about giving advice to others.

• Listen attentively to the other members of the group so as to learn from their insights. The words of the Bible affect each person in a different way, so a group provides a wealth of understanding for each member.

• Don't fear silence. Silence in a group is as important as silence in personal study. It allows individuals time to listen to the voice of God's Spirit and the opportunity to form their thoughts before they speak.

• Solicit several responses for each question. The thoughts of different people will build on the answers of others and will lead to deeper insights for all.

• Don't fear controversy. Differences of opinions are a sign of a healthy and honest group. If you cannot resolve an issue, continue on, agreeing to disagree. There is probably some truth in each viewpoint.

• Discuss the questions that seem most important for the group. There is no need to cover all the questions in the group session.

• Realize that some questions about the Bible cannot be resolved, even by experts. Don't get stuck on some issue for which there are no clear answers.

• Whatever is said in the group is said in confidence and should be regarded as such.

• Pray as a group in whatever way feels comfortable. Pray for the members of your group throughout the week.

Schedule for group study

Session 1: Introduction   Date: _____

Session 2: Lessons 1–6   Date: _____

Session 3: Lessons 7–12   Date: _____

Session 4: Lessons 13–18   Date: _____

Session 5: Lessons 19–24   Date: _____

Session 6: Lessons 25–30   Date: _____

The earth is the Lord's and all that is in it, the world, and those who live in it. Ps 24:1

Stewardship of the Earth

For centuries people have had the ability to look outward from the earth at the planets and stars in the universe with the aid of telescopes. But only in recent decades have we had the ability to look at the earth itself from the perspective of outer space. This image of the earth as a blue-green orb, with its verdant vegetation and deep azure seas, surrounded by a misty atmosphere, has become a sacred icon for people of our day. It is a reflection of the goodness and grandeur of its Creator, a reminder that our world is a beautiful place, a friendly habitat, and a blessed creation.

The faith expressed by the biblical writers recognizes the world as God's good creation. The world belongs to God and humanity is God's steward, responsible to God for the care of creation. Preserving the resources of the earth and protecting its creatures are essential aspects of a human life faithfully bonded with God. Being a steward of the earth by living in harmony with the world's other creatures is a joyful privilege that flows from a right relationship with God. Viewing the earth as a divine gift leads to a deep and personal desire to care for that gift and to pass it on to forthcoming generations.

Our modern life often keeps us isolated from the natural wonders of our world. Surrounded by manufactured environments, insulated in our urban homes and offices, eating prepackaged foods, we may rarely have the opportunity to encounter the wild and awesome wonder of the earth's grandeur.

1

When we stand at the edge of a cliff with a roaring surf below, pause in an ancient forest at the foot of a giant hardwood, look out upon a dew-sparkled meadow at sunrise, we place ourselves in the situations which have engendered awe-filled reverence for the Creator and for creation through the ages. By reflecting on these kinds of experiences and by listening to the Scriptures that speak of the wonders of creation, we can nurture within our hearts a love for the natural world and a passion for its care.

In the face of the earth's ecological crisis, mostly we know what we have to do but we lack the will to do it. For this reason, many have concluded that working out the current crisis is as much a religious challenge as a political one. Our tendency to use the world's resources to gratify our selfish desires is a temptation that can be overcome with a changed spiritual viewpoint. A religious approach to caring for the earth teaches us reverence for creation and shows us how to base our attitudes and actions on God's revelation. Studying the Scriptures moves us toward a deeper awareness of the created world and appreciation of its meaning and blessing. Rather than seeking meaning by rapaciously consuming the gifts entrusted to us, we can find spiritual fulfillment through respectful engagement with the beauty of the earth.

Reflection and discussion

• What experiences have given me a deeper respect and reverence for the earth?

• In what way is the ecological crisis which faces the earth a spiritual and religious problem? In what way could studying the Bible help?

God's Awesome Yet Fragile World

The earth is a delicate series of balanced systems and processes which support and nurture all of life. Surrounding our beloved emerald and azure globe is a fragile layer of vapor and gases that protects and supports the wonderful fabric of life called the biosphere. Some gases absorb the energy of the sun and regulate its warmth while other elements shield the earth from the sun's destructive radiation. Because of the tilt of the earth and its continual rotation, the atmosphere circulates, the oceans create currents, and the seasons change. Moisture is continually recycled and purified through evaporation and the rain and snow irrigate the earth in regular cycles. Water is also naturally filtered through the flow of streams and rivers, making it habitable and drinkable for earth's creatures. The soil is nurtured and renewed through a cyclical process as decaying organisms and other elements support a growing fabric of vegetation.

The biosphere is comprised of many communities of organisms in their diverse environments called ecosystems. Forests, glades, marshes, prairies, lakes, and oceans are all places of wondrous environmental harmony. The animals, plants, soils, and climates of each system all interact as an integrated ecological unit. In each natural system, diverse species of life flourish and reproduce from one generation to the next. The wondrous balance exhibited in each natural environment requires respect for its intricate complexity.

Though we are able to investigate and understand the natural world in a way that was impossible for our ancestors, we recognize with them that creation declares the wisdom and glory of God. God lovingly provides the rains and the seasons, gives food and flowing water for the creatures, and satisfies the earth. God's eternal power and divine nature are understood and seen through the beauty and abundance of the things God has made.

Yet, in our day, living creatures, and the air, soil, and water that support them, face unprecedented threats. Many of these perils are global; most stem directly from human activity. Economies that seek to maximize immediate returns at the expense of long-term sustainability are becoming the norm throughout the world. The current practices of humanity may so alter the living world in the future that it will be unable to sustain the delicately balanced systems required for life to flourish.

Threats to the atmosphere include toxic emissions that fill the air, depletion of the protective ozone, and an unprecedented buildup of greenhouse gases causing rising temperatures and climate changes. Perils to the earth's waters include dangerous chemicals discharged into rivers, toxic leaks trickling into the groundwater, and abundant waste dumped into seas and oceans. Land abuse includes destruction of tropical forests, devastation of natural habitats, and the ruin of creation's natural fertility with pesticides and herbicides. As a result, the variety of earth's species is diminishing and creatures that once thrived in their habitats have died.

We must learn that creation is not humanity's possession. It is entrusted to humanity for its tending and safekeeping. Exercising responsible stewardship means pursuing simpler lifestyles. It means seeking contentment in those things that will sustain us, and not grasping more and more from the earth for our own selfish advancement. Sustainable living means providing an acceptable quality of life for the present generation without compromising that of future generations. Caring for the earth means taking into account all of our fellow creatures, leaving for them what is naturally theirs and allowing creation to heal, to restore its fruitfulness, and to praise its Creator.

Reflection and discussion

• What do I know about the ecosystems near where I live? What are the trees, birds, fish, and other wildlife that share my habitat?

• How would I rate my own personal stewardship of creation? What do I do well to care for the earth, and what can I do better?

Biblical Perspectives on Ecology

The Bible offers a rich foundation for environmental consciousness. Some have accused the Christian tradition of fostering apathy for the material world by orienting people toward an immaterial existence in a spiritual heaven. But a review of biblical texts shows us that the world is not something from which we should try to escape. Both the ancient literature of Israel and the writings of the early church demonstrate that God's original intentions for creation as well as God's plan for creation's future fulfillment are centered in the world of bodily, worldly reality.

The psalms and wisdom literature of Israel rejoice in the created world. They present the world in all of its diversity as a gift from God in which all creatures delight. Singing the psalms convinces us that the non-human world is precious in God's eyes quite apart from any usefulness to humanity. The skies and the birds that fill it, the seas and the creatures that swim the deep, and the land with all of its vegetation and animals exist in a wonderful harmony in which each creature contributes to the good of the others. The book of Job and the other wisdom writings demonstrate that God's purposes for the world reach far beyond the understanding and control of humans. God loves his creation and watches over and sustains it with utmost care. Humans exist as an integral part of creation, yet God desires that people live wisely, in a way that contributes to the created world with respect for its meaning and goodness.

The opening chapters of Genesis present God's original design for the world. Every part of material reality comes from the loving hand of its Creator who declares it very good. Within this diverse and magnificent creation God fashioned his masterpiece, made in the divine image. Humankind was entrusted with the task of stewardship of the earth, charged with preserving and protecting what God had made. Even when man and woman abandoned their task, their responsibility remained. God made an everlasting covenant, not only with humankind, but with every living creature on the earth. The rainbow would be the sign in every generation of God's commitment to the earth.

Because the sinful tendencies within human beings lead to greedy consumption and callous exploitation of God's creatures, the law and prophets of Israel established commands and boundaries to encourage respect for God's gifts. The weekly Sabbath requiring rest for all creatures and the Sabbath year for the regeneration of the land promote a lifestyle that honors the natural rhythms and cycles of the earth. The prophets condemn abuse of the earth's resources and continue offering hope for a time when God would restore creation to its wholeness.

The gospels proclaim that God loved the world so much that the divine Word became flesh and lived within it. He delighted in the natural world, taught about the seeds, flowers, and birds, retreated to the mountains to pray, and calmed the storms on the sea. And finally he rose bodily from death and assured his followers of complete victory over every brokenness and bondage.

The Christian Scriptures proclaim that God's saving will is complete restoration of the whole creation. Not only will God raise people to the fullness of life, but the entire world will be redeemed from the bondage of futility and decay. The risen Christ is the world's first experience of God's eventual renewal of the whole cosmos. The last book of the Bible returns to images from Scripture's first book, depicting a renewed and fruitful earth. The images of a fertile garden with the tree of life watered by a pure, flowing river express God's original intentions for the earth which will inevitably be fulfilled.

These wondrous images that fill the Bible's sacred texts demonstrate that God loves the world so much that he will never abandon it and will eventually restore its broken beauty. These texts teach us the responsibility of stewardship and offer us abiding hope. If God loves the world so much, then so must we. We must not abuse and destroy what is so precious to God. The Scriptures call us to be environmental stewards, people who joyfully and lovingly care for God's good creation.

Reflection and discussion

• Some heretical teachers in the early centuries of Christianity taught that the physical world was evil and the goal of life was to escape from material reality. How does the Bible demonstrate this teaching to be false?

• What does it mean to love the world as God loves it? How do I demonstrate a love for creation?

The Practical Challenge of Stewardship

The challenge of environmental stewardship is to put what we know and what we believe into practice. As individuals and families, we must examine our energy consumption and water usage, our garbage and recycling practices, and our lifestyle choices and decisions as consumers. We should consider how we pass on a respect and appreciation for God's creation to the next generation and how we can instill hope in young people that a more sustainable world is worth struggling to achieve.

Within our society we must move beyond short-sighted policies that increase production but harm the earth. In business, labor, and government, we must support the common good, considering not only the environmental needs of the present generation but also those of future generations. All decision-making regarding the use of the earth's resources ought to pass the ethical test of sustainability so that resources are not depleted or damaged for the future.

The contribution of the church is critical in raising awareness of environmental concerns. It must issue the prophetic call for a change of heart on the issues that threaten our world. The challenge to stewardship of the earth should be communicated in the preaching, worship, and educational programs of Christian communities. Studying the Scriptures helps people understand that our planetary home is sacred, and what people regard as sacred is more likely to be treated with care and respect.

We need today a joint commitment by science and religion to preserve the earth. Science tells us what we need to do; religion tells us why we need to do it. Science has not demystified the natural world. Rather, the more we understand its intricacy and extravagance, the more we are able to contemplate its mystery. Religion and science have different roles to perform in the work of caring for the earth, but drawing on the insights of both, humanity can figure out how to live in harmony with all the creatures of the earth. Then we can continue to enjoy the intoxicating beauty of the sunset, the amazing power of the roaring sea, the exquisite loveliness of the butterfly, and the delicate perfection of the blooming flower. Then nature can continue to amaze us with its miracles.

Reflection and discussion

• In what practical challenge facing the world can I make a difference? What step can I take first?

• How can religion and science become partners in the work of preserving the earth? Why do we need the contributions of both?

A New Ecological Spirituality

A spirituality that reflects the biblical understanding of the created world requires a deep humility. It admits that the earth was not created merely for human use, but to give glory to God. Such a spirituality calls for a profound respect and reverence in the face of creation's sacredness. It recognizes that humanity did not weave the web of life, but that we are strands within it. It realizes that ultimately, "the earth is the Lord's" (Ps 24:1).

Our spiritual ancestors, like most traditional peoples of the world, possessed this type of respectful awe for the natural world. Their psalms called upon the worshiping assembly to join with all the elements of creation to offer praise to God. They acknowledged their spiritual kinship with God's other creatures, and they knew that these creatures always give God glory just by being what they were created to be. In previous ages, the praise of all creation had a much more important place in the prayer and liturgy of the temple and the church. But this ecological spirituality is being renewed in our day and will no doubt continue to affect the content of our prayer and the form of our worship.

Francis of Assisi is a wonderful model for the humility and reverence for creation that is being birthed again today. He evangelized not only the human inhabitants of his medieval world but also the birds and the wolves. In his prayer to God, Francis deposed humanity from any exclusive focus of concern and praised God with all his creaturely kin. He addressed the creatures of the world as his family—brother sun and sister moon, brother wind and sister water, brother fire and sister earth. His Canticle of Creation can inspire us to look at creation with new eyes and see within its beauty, as through filigree, the love of God.

Prayer

Thank you, Creator God, for the world you have given to us. Thank you for its beauty and wonders and for the witness it offers of your power and love. I ask you to help me reflect your image on the earth by treating your creation with care and affection. As I read these sacred Scriptures, give me a new respect for the earth and a new understanding of my responsibilities as your steward. Help me serve you with humility and treat with reverence the sacred gifts you have given to me.

SUGGESTIONS FOR FACILITATORS, GROUP SESSION 1

1. If the group is meeting for the first time, or if there are newcomers joining the group, it is helpful to provide nametags.

2. Distribute the books to the members of the group.

3. You may want to ask the participants to introduce themselves and tell the group a bit about themselves.

4. Ask one or more of these introductory questions:
   • What drew you to join this group?
   • What is your biggest fear in beginning this Bible study?
   • How is beginning this study like a "threshold" for you?

5. You may want to pray this prayer as a group:

Come upon us, Holy Spirit, to enlighten and guide us as we begin this study on our stewardship of your creation. You have given us this world and all its creatures along with the privilege of caring for them. Motivate us to read the Scriptures and give us a deeper love for God's word each day so that we will better understand your will for creation. Work deeply within us so that we will join with all creation in worshiping our Creator. Bless us during this session and throughout the coming week with the fire of your love.

6. Read the Introduction aloud, pausing at each question for discussion. Group members may wish to write the insights of the group as each question is discussed. Encourage several members of the group to respond to each question.

7. Don't feel compelled to finish the complete Introduction during the session. It is better to allow sufficient time to talk about the questions raised than to rush to the end. Group members may read any remaining sections on their own after the group meeting.

8. Instruct group members to read the first six lessons on their own during the six days before the next group meeting. They should write out their own answers to the questions as preparation for next week's group discussion.

9. Fill in the date for each group meeting under "Schedule for Group Study."

10. Conclude by praying aloud together the prayer at the end of the Introduction.

When I look at your heavens, the work of your fingers,
the moon and the stars that you have established;
what are human beings that you are mindful of them,
mortals that you care for them? Ps 8:3–4

God's Majesty and Humanity's Dignity

PSALM 8

¹*O Lord, our Sovereign,*
  how majestic is your name in all the earth!

You have set your glory above the heavens.
  ²*Out of the mouths of babes and infants*
you have founded a bulwark because of your foes,
  to silence the enemy and the avenger.
³*When I look at your heavens, the work of your fingers,*
  the moon and the stars that you have established;
⁴*what are human beings that you are mindful of them,*
  mortals that you care for them?

⁵*Yet you have made them a little lower than God,*
  and crowned them with glory and honor.
⁶*You have given them dominion over the works of your hands;*
  you have put all things under their feet,

⁷all sheep and oxen,
and also the beasts of the field,
⁸the birds of the air, and the fish of the sea,
whatever passes along the paths of the seas.

⁹O Lord, our Sovereign,
how majestic is your name in all the earth!

The psalms are the hymnbook of ancient Israel, inviting us to enter a long tradition of praise to God. Psalm 8 is a wonderful example of what a hymn should be, celebrating who God is and what God has done, all in a spirit of awe and wonder. The hymn is addressed completely to God, beginning and ending with an exclamation of God's sovereign rule over the cosmos (verses 1, 9). God's supreme majesty is evident in all creation, and our rightful response is to cry out in praise and worship.

Gazing at the moon and the stars, the vastness of the night sky can lead us to a feeling of insignificance (verse 3). With wonderful poetic imagery, the psalmist describes God's arrangement of the heavenly bodies as the work of God's "fingers," the handiwork of the divine artisan. Within such a magnificent creation, the singer asks, "What are human beings that you are mindful of them, mortals that you care for them?" (verse 4). Who are we in relation to the grandeur of the heavens or the majesty of God? Communal worship of our transcendent God offers us a healthy dose of humility in the face of the awesome wonder of creation.

Though small and insignificant from the standpoint of human rationality, from the view of God's revelation human beings have a special and unique place in the order of creation. In God's plan our value is incomparable. We have been made "a little lower than God" (verse 5), placed between God and his other creatures, as stewards of creation. In fact, human beings have been given a share in God's royal rule, "crowned" with honor and glory, the regal traits of God. Though minuscule in comparison with the Creator and his wondrous works, earthly mortals are appointed to represent God's reign to other creatures.

This divinely appointed task for humanity to serve as God's royal regent in the world is described as "dominion" over the works of God's hands (verse 6).

Humans are endowed by God with tremendous dignity and remarkable responsibility in regard to the other creatures of the world. The sphere of this dominion is over all living creatures, both domesticated and wild animals (verse 7) as well as the birds of the air and the fish of the sea (verse 8). Yet, human authority over creation is far from absolute. It is a power exercised only at the behest of the Sovereign, a control that must reflect the purposes of the Creator. Dominion is nothing less than representing the reign of God in the world.

Human dominion over creation has been misunderstood and abused through the ages. Dominion has become domination, and humanity has misconstrued the tremendous privilege of serving as God's viceroy in the world and taken it as an excuse to use its rule for ruin. This psalm of praise to God's majesty challenges us to think again about our dignity and our accountability as representatives of God's rule within creation. This hymn to creation's Sovereign reminds us that our supremacy in the natural world is subordinate to the One who reigns over the cosmos.

Reflection and discussion

• What natural experiences have been powerful reminders to me of God's sovereign majesty?

• In what sense does gazing at a star-studded sky lead me to feel both my insignificance in the cosmos and my dignity in God's eyes?

• Why does it mean to say that human beings have dominion over the other creatures of the earth?

• How has the privilege of humanity expressed in verses 5–6 been misunderstood, leading to destructive abuse of creation?

• In what way do I feel important to God?

Prayer

O Lord, our Sovereign, when I look at the vast beauty of your creation I marvel at the dignity and calling you have given to me. As a steward of your earth, help me care for your creatures and embody your reign in the world.

Let the heavens be glad, and let the earth rejoice;
let the sea roar, and all that fills it; let the field exult, and everything in it.
Then shall all the trees of the forest sing for joy. Ps 96:11–12

All Creatures Sing
Praises to God

PSALM 96

¹O sing to the Lord a new song;
  sing to the Lord, all the earth.
²Sing to the Lord, bless his name;
  tell of his salvation from day to day.
³Declare his glory among the nations,
  his marvelous works among all the peoples.
⁴For great is the Lord, and greatly to be praised;
  he is to be revered above all gods.
⁵For all the gods of the peoples are idols,
  but the Lord made the heavens.
⁶Honor and majesty are before him;
  strength and beauty are in his sanctuary.
⁷Ascribe to the Lord, O families of the peoples,
  ascribe to the Lord glory and strength.
⁸Ascribe to the Lord the glory due his name;
  bring an offering, and come into his courts.

⁹*Worship the Lord in holy splendor;*
tremble before him, all the earth.

¹⁰*Say among the nations, "The Lord is king!*
The world is firmly established; it shall never be moved.
He will judge the peoples with equity."
¹¹*Let the heavens be glad, and let the earth rejoice;*
let the sea roar, and all that fills it;
¹²*let the field exult, and everything in it.*
Then shall all the trees of the forest sing for joy
¹³*before the Lord; for he is coming,*
for he is coming to judge the earth.
He will judge the world with righteousness,
and the peoples with his truth.

This psalm is a great universal summons to praise God. "All the earth" is called to sing a hymn of praise to God in a grand symphony of creation. All the creatures of the earth, each in their own way, sing of God's salvation, his glory, and his marvelous works (verses 2–3). The whole cosmos reverberates with praise.

Following the summons to sing to the Lord, bless his name, and declare his glory, the psalmist expresses the reasons for this call: God is great and worthy of great praise (verse 4). The Lord is to be revered above all would-be gods or whatever other powers people worship and trust. Most of the nations of the ancient world worshiped the heavenly bodies, but God's worthiness to be praised lies in his work as the Creator of all: "the Lord made the heavens" (verse 5). Therefore, all the attributes of divine kingship can be ascribed to God: honor, majesty, strength, beauty, and especially glory (verses 6–8).

The primary message that all the earth is summoned to acclaim is this: the Lord is king—God reigns over all of creation (verse 10). This royal king has firmly established the world with an order in both nature and society that can be trusted. The same Lord who created the world also comes to judge the world with equity, righteousness, and truth (verses 10, 13). All the earth can look backward to creation and forward to judgment with confident trust because the Lord reigns.

Because we mistakenly think that divine judgment will be a day of gloom and doom, it might sound strange to us that the impending judgment of God is described here as a cause for rejoicing. But here God's judging the world with equity, righteousness, and truth means restoring the world to order and harmony. As God sets things right, the world is restored. So, not only do the people sing praise, but the heavens are glad and the earth rejoices (verse 11). Everything in creation is joyful, each in its own way: the sea and all its creatures roar, the field and all the creatures within it exult, and "all the trees of the forest sing for joy" (verses 11–12).

This symphony of creation shows the natural connectedness of all the elements of the created world. The social order of humanity and the created order of nature are intertwined in a deep ecological bond. Throughout the biblical literature, this interconnected harmony and peace in the world is called the kingdom of God or God's reign. It is God's desire for the world, the way the world ought to be.

Reflection and discussion

• In what way do humans sometimes prevent creatures of the earth from offering their natural praise to God?

• How can we allow all creatures of the earth to praise God?

• In what ways does human worship of God parallel the worship by God's other creatures?

• How can I include the natural elements of the world in my praise of God?

• Why is God's coming to judge the earth a cause for rejoicing? What new understanding of the final judgment does this offer to me?

Prayer

Royal Lord, you have made the heavens and the earth, and all creation sings your praise. Deepen my reverence for all the creatures of the world so that I can join with the roaring sea and the singing trees of the forest in a symphony of praise to you.

You make springs gush forth in the valleys; they flow between the hills, giving drink to every wild animal; the wild asses quench their thirst. Ps 104:10–11

God Sustains and Cares for Creation

PSALM 104:1–13

¹Bless the Lord, O my soul.
　O Lord my God, you are very great.
　You are clothed with honor and majesty,
　　²wrapped in light as with a garment.
　You stretch out the heavens like a tent,
　　³you set the beams of your chambers on the waters,
　you make the clouds your chariot,
　　you ride on the wings of the wind,
　⁴you make the winds your messengers,
　　fire and flame your ministers.

⁵You set the earth on its foundations,
　so that it shall never be shaken.
⁶You cover it with the deep as with a garment;
　the waters stood above the mountains.
⁷At your rebuke they flee;
　at the sound of your thunder they take to flight.

⁸*They rose up to the mountains, ran down to the valleys
to the place that you appointed for them.*
⁹*You set a boundary that they may not pass,
so that they might not again cover the earth.*

¹⁰*You make springs gush forth in the valleys;
they flow between the hills,*
¹¹*giving drink to every wild animal;
the wild asses quench their thirst.*
¹²*By the streams the birds of the air have their habitation;
they sing among the branches.*
¹³*From your lofty abode you water the mountains;
the earth is satisfied with the fruit of your work.*

Psalm 104 is a magnificent, thirty-five verse hymn of praise for all the marvels of the created world. The psalm is full of wonder and joy as the poet contemplates the goodness of creation and the personal concern that God shows in promoting the life and order of the world. It begins and ends with a call to glorify God: "Bless the Lord, O my soul. Praise the Lord!" (verses 1, 35). Between these verses is the poet's contemplation of the Creator's majesty and creation's harmonious order and connectedness.

The psalmist describes the Creator with imagery indicating that God transcends the world and is also intimately involved in the world. The royal God is clothed in light, building his splendid residence on the waters of the sky, using the clouds as his chariot and the winds and lightning of the thunderstorm as his attendants (verses 2–4). Where we may see merely a threatening front of clouds crossing the sky, the psalm enlarges our perspective to see a manifestation of God's power.

The poet continues this mythological imagery, connecting creation with God's transcendent power. The Creator established the earth securely, though the deep waters covered the earth, even above the mountains (verses 5–6). But God banished the waters so that the mountains and valleys emerged, and he confined the waters to their appointed place so they would not return to cover the earth (verses 7–9). In this creation account the world is shown to be reliable and secure because the Lord reigns. The account is less about what God created, and more about how God's authority produces the order and rhythms of the world.

God uses his control of the world to provide for the life and welfare of all creatures. Not only has the Lord bounded the waters of the deep so they do not destroy life; God has channeled them into springs and streams to provide drink and refreshment for the wild animals and the birds of the air (verses 10–12). These same waters God has directed into the refreshing rains that water the earth and bring forth vegetation and fruit (verse 13).

God did not merely bring the world into being and then leave it alone. The world exists because of the Creator's continuous care and sustenance. All earth's creatures depend upon God, and God provides for them through the wondrously interconnected system of the natural world.

Reflection and discussion

• Which images suggest that God transcends the natural world? Which suggest that God is intimately involved with the world?

• In what way has the scientific worldview of our day added to our sense of wonder at the natural world?

Prayer

Creator God, all that exists comes from your creative design. I marvel at the harmonious order and rhythm of the world you have made. May I praise you always for the goodness that is so evident in the world around me.

The trees of the Lord are watered abundantly,
the cedars of Lebanon that he planted. In them the birds build their nests;
the stork has its home in the fir trees. Ps 104:16–17

A Wondrously Interrelated World

PSALM 104:14–23

¹⁴*You cause the grass to grow for the cattle,*
and plants for people to use,
to bring forth food from the earth,
    ¹⁵*and wine to gladden the human heart,*
oil to make the face shine,
    and bread to strengthen the human heart.
¹⁶*The trees of the Lord are watered abundantly,*
    the cedars of Lebanon that he planted.
¹⁷*In them the birds build their nests;*
    the stork has its home in the fir trees.
¹⁸*The high mountains are for the wild goats;*
    the rocks are a refuge for the coneys.
¹⁹*You have made the moon to mark the seasons;*
    the sun knows its time for setting.
²⁰*You make darkness, and it is night,*
    when all the animals of the forest come creeping out.

²¹ *The young lions roar for their prey,*
seeking their food from God.
²² *When the sun rises, they withdraw*
and lie down in their dens.
²³ *People go out to their work*
and to their labor until the evening.

T he poet continues to describe how God gives the creatures of the earth what is good for their life. The details portray a wondrously interrelated world which is a place of beauty, delight, and blessing. Cattle are fed, trees are watered, birds nest, goats climb the mountains, badgers take shelter in the rocks, and humans relax with wine and refresh their skin with oil (verses 14–18). All the diverse types of creatures fit together into a harmonious whole.

The cycles of the moon indicate the changing seasons, and the sun rises and sets to mark the rhythm of the day and night. Sun and moon alternate so that wild lions can roar and prowl at night and people can labor during the day until evening (verses 19–23). Because each follows the natural cycle of the day and night, they are not a threat to one another.

As part of God's good creation, the human being is simply one creature among the many sustained by God's care. The creatures of the world are valuable not just because of their usefulness to humans; they are valuable to one another. The cedars are valuable for the birds to build their nests, the fir trees for the storks to create a home, and the mountains as refuge for the wild goats. One part of creation cares for another because of the ongoing care that God built into the ecological systems of the earth. The rocks and trees, birds and wild animals are valuable in their own right simply because they are God's creation.

Food, water, habitat, topography, and the change of days and seasons all form an intricate system in which creatures live. When people cultivate the land to bring forth food from the earth and build on the land to bring forth civilization, they must do so in harmony with the needs of the other creatures. Disrupting the food sources of wild animals, the flow of water, the habitat of birds and creatures, or the topography of the earth is to violate an intricate ecosystem that provides for all God's creatures. The human creatures must know that they are integrated into an interdependent world. They depend not only on God, but on all the other creatures and elements of the earth.

Reflection and discussion

• What natural setting have I seen that portrays the beauty and interdependence of the earth's creatures?

• What are other examples in which the creatures of the earth are valuable to one another and care for one another because God's care is built into the ecological systems?

• In what way do humans disrupt the food sources and habitats of other creatures, violating the intricate ecosystem which provides for all of God's creatures?

Prayer

Provident God, you care for all the creatures of the earth and provide for their needs. Help me be more aware of the needs of the other living things on the earth and realize the interdependence of all your creation.

When you take away their breath, they die and return to their dust.
When you send forth your spirit, they are created;
and you renew the face of the ground. Ps 104:29–30

All Creatures Rejoice in Their Maker's Wisdom

PSALM 104:24–35

²⁴O Lord, how manifold are your works!
    In wisdom you have made them all;
    the earth is full of your creatures.
²⁵Yonder is the sea, great and wide,
    creeping things innumerable are there,
    living things both small and great.
²⁶There go the ships,
    and Leviathan that you formed to sport in it.

²⁷These all look to you
    to give them their food in due season;
²⁸when you give to them, they gather it up;
    when you open your hand, they are filled with good things.
²⁹When you hide your face, they are dismayed;
    when you take away their breath, they die
    and return to their dust.

³⁰When you send forth your spirit, they are created;
and you renew the face of the ground.

³¹May the glory of the Lord endure forever;
may the Lord rejoice in his works—
³²who looks on the earth and it trembles,
who touches the mountains and they smoke.
³³I will sing to the Lord as long as I live;
I will sing praise to my God while I have being.
³⁴May my meditation be pleasing to him,
for I rejoice in the Lord.
³⁵Let sinners be consumed from the earth,
and let the wicked be no more.
Bless the Lord, O my soul.
Praise the Lord!

The inventory of the earth's creatures in the previous section of the psalm is just a sampling of the variety of inanimate and living beings that fill God's world. This last section of the psalm begins with an exclamation of astonishment at how many diverse creatures the Lord has made: "O Lord, how manifold are your works!" (verse 24). For the poet, this variety and intricacy within creation is a display of God's wisdom. There is a reverence here for the world of nature, as the psalmist sees God sustaining and caring for life within the multiplicity of living things.

Having already poetically expressed the wonders of earth and sky, the psalmist turns to the vast sea as another arena of God's creative care (verses 25–26). Even this deep underwater world is teeming with creatures beyond number. All of these marine animals, both small and great, look to God to feed and sustain them through the ecological system of the world's oceans and seas. Humans become creatures of the sea as they travel by ship in harmony with the other denizens of the depths. As on the land, the human being is simply one creature among the many in the deep, blue sea, not dominating or destroying, but calmly floating among the occupants of the ocean.

Because God is the creator and sustainer of all, the creatures depend upon God for food (verses 27–28) and for life itself (verses 29–30). The natural growth cycles of organisms in the environment and the natural process of creatures feeding off of others is God's gift. The rhythm of life and death and the appearance of new life is also God's gift. It is the effect of the relationship between the breath/spirit of creatures and the breath/spirit of God. The life-giving breath of God, which animates the human being according to Genesis 2:7, also creates all living creatures and renews the earth with life (verse 30). This understanding implies an intimate unity among all living creatures, as all are animated with the same divine life-breath.

The psalm concludes with a series of expressed hopes. "The glory of the Lord" (verse 31) is the way God is revealed in the splendor of the created world. As the Lord sustains the world, the earth in turn reveals God. The psalmist wishes that the radiance of God be continually revealed through the beauty and intricacy of the natural world. The psalm also expresses hope that the Lord "rejoice in his work," as the singer rejoices in the Lord (verses 33–34). Just as other psalms show that God grieves with our sorrows, God is not above expressing joy with his creation.

God's desire for the world is the banishment of evil. The harmony of creation and its beautiful panorama is disrupted by the flaw of human sin. Though the psalmist's final wish that the wicked be banished from the earth seems discordant within this lovely hymn (verse 35), it actually springs from the singer's hope for a peaceful world, an earth in which God's justice is manifest and sin is no more. This, too, is God's final plan for creation. The wicked defy God's sovereignty when they deny their dependence on the natural systems through which God provides for the earth's creatures and when they imagine themselves autonomous and distinct from the natural world and its creatures.

We are slowly learning that we damage ourselves and threaten the future of life when we live in alienation from the matrix of God's creation to which we belong. When we sing the psalms of praise, we broaden our perspective. We become accountable to our transcendent Lord and envision ourselves within the tender care of our creative and rejoicing God.

Reflection and discussion

• What new perspective on the world does praying Psalm 104 offer me?

• In what way is the diversity and multiplicity of living things an expression of God's wisdom?

• What are some examples of human autonomy which alienate us from the rest of creation?

Prayer

O Lord, how many and diverse are the works of your creation. On land, in sky and sea, we see your creative work. May my breathing in and out remind me that my life is a gift from you which I share with the living creatures of our world.

Mountains and all hills, fruit trees and all cedars!
Wild animals and all cattle, creeping things and flying birds! Ps 148:9–10

All Creation Sings Praises to God

PSALM 148

¹*Praise the Lord!*
Praise the Lord from the heavens;
  praise him in the heights!
²*Praise him, all his angels;*
  praise him, all his host!
³*Praise him, sun and moon;*
  praise him, all you shining stars!
⁴*Praise him, you highest heavens,*
  and you waters above the heavens!

⁵*Let them praise the name of the Lord,*
  for he commanded and they were created.
⁶*He established them forever and ever;*
  he fixed their bounds, which cannot be passed.

⁷*Praise the Lord from the earth,*
  you sea monsters and all deeps,
⁸*fire and hail, snow and frost,*
  stormy wind fulfilling his command!

⁹*Mountains and all hills,*
fruit trees and all cedars!
¹⁰*Wild animals and all cattle,*
creeping things and flying birds!

¹¹*Kings of the earth and all peoples,*
princes and all rulers of the earth!
¹²*Young men and women alike,*
old and young together!
¹³*Let them praise the name of the Lord,*
for his name alone is exalted;
his glory is above earth and heaven.
¹⁴*He has raised up a horn for his people,*
praise for all his faithful,
for the people of Israel who are close to him.
Praise the Lord!

This glorious hymn is an invitation for all creation to join in the praise of God. This cosmic worship is composed of two great choirs: one "from the heavens" (verses 1–6) and the other "from the earth" (verses 7–14). In this vision of reality, the heavens and the earth are the two realms that constitute the cosmos. Each choir is urged to give glory to God the Creator: "Let them praise the name of the Lord" (verses 5, 13).

Representatives from every part of the created world are summoned to sing God's praises. The heavenly creatures include the angels, sun, moon, stars, and clouds (verses 2–4). Their grandeur proclaims the glory of God, and they respond to their call to praise God by shining forth in all their radiance. The reason for their praise is profoundly simple: God has created them and continues to govern them (verses 5–6).

The earthly creatures include the creatures of the sea and the ocean depths (verse 7). They encompass the various meteorological phenomena that affect the earth: lightning, hail, snow, frost, winds, and storms (verse 8). The panorama of creation incorporates the mountains, hills, fruit trees, cedars, wild and domestic animals, creatures that crawl on the earth, and birds that fly in the air (verses 9–10). Finally, humans join in the praise. Designated as royal rulers and peoples, men and women, old and young, all are equal in God's sight despite office, gender, or age (verses 11–12). Like that of the heavens, the reason for the earth's praise is also profound and clear: "his name alone is exalted; his glory is above heaven and earth" (verse 13).

Those who were close to God, his people Israel, experienced power and purpose when they joined in the universal praise of God (verse 14). Like most people of the ancient world, they had a profound respect and reverence for the natural world in which they lived. Unlike our consumer culture of today, which tends to regard the elements of the natural world as something to be put to human use, ancient peoples had a respectful fear of the forces of nature. They instinctively knew that if they lived in harmony with the natural laws that govern the world, the earth would yield its riches and their well-being would be assured.

From the perspective of faith, praise of God is at the heart of the universe and is the core purpose of every created being. As human beings, sometimes we limit our praise to our own immediate circumstances and to what God has done specifically for ourselves. But the psalms broaden our perspective as they testify to the praiseworthiness of the Lord in every moment by every creature. Situating ourselves within the vastness of all creation's worship, we discover within ourselves a reverent wonder for who God truly is. We realize the narrow vision of a culture that looks only to human profits from the earth and understand more fully the marvelous dignity of being a creature of God.

Reflection and discussion

• In what way does joining this cosmic symphony broaden my perspective?

• The psalm assumes that all the elements of creation know how to praise God. How do mountains, trees, and wild animals praise God?

• In what way did the peoples of the ancient world exhibit a respect for the natural world that we have lost today?

• In what way does this psalm undermine our modern world's destructive culture? In what way can the psalm be healing for our society?

Prayer

Majestic Lord, your glory is above earth and heaven. May all creation praise your power, and may I join the universe in exalting your holy name. As you have entrusted humanity with care for the earth, may we live as worthy stewards of your creation.

SUGGESTIONS FOR FACILITATORS, GROUP SESSION 2

1. If there are newcomers who were not present for the first group session, introduce them now.

2. You may want to pray this prayer as a group:

Lord God of all creation, all your works manifest your goodness and love. The psalms of the Scriptures teach us how to honor you and give you thanks for all the gifts of creation. Give me the voice and the desire to sing your praises along with my ancestors in faith and with all the other creatures of the earth. I praise you for the beauty, harmony, and variety of life in our world. Give me a desire to protect and nurture the creatures of the earth so that they will always reflect your magnificent love and give you glory.

3. Ask one or both of the following questions:
   • What was your biggest challenge in Bible study over this past week?
   • What did you learn about yourself this week?

4. Discuss lessons 1 through 6 together. Assuming that group members have read the Scripture and commentary during the week, there is no need to read it aloud. As you review each lesson, you might want to briefly summarize the Scripture passages of each lesson and ask the group what stands out most clearly from the commentary.

5. Choose one or more of the questions for reflection and discussion from each lesson to talk over as a group. You may want to ask group members which question was most challenging or helpful to them as you review each lesson.

6. Keep the discussion moving, but don't rush the discussion in order to complete more questions. Allow time for the questions that provoke the most discussion.

7. Instruct group members to complete lessons 7 through 12 on their own during the six days before the next group meeting. They should write out their own answers to the questions as preparation for next week's group discussion.

8. Conclude by praying aloud together the prayer at the end of lesson 6, or any other prayer you choose.

"Where were you when I laid the foundation of the earth?
Tell me, if you have understanding. Who determined its measurements—
surely you know!" Job 38:4–5

God's Fierce and Beautiful Creativity

JOB 38:1–27

Then the Lord answered Job out of the whirlwind:
²"Who is this that darkens counsel by words without knowledge?
³Gird up your loins like a man,
I will question you, and you shall declare to me.

⁴"Where were you when I laid the foundation of the earth?
Tell me, if you have understanding.
⁵Who determined its measurements—surely you know!
Or who stretched the line upon it?
⁶On what were its bases sunk,
or who laid its cornerstone
⁷when the morning stars sang together
and all the heavenly beings shouted for joy?

⁸"Or who shut in the sea with doors
when it burst out from the womb?—
⁹when I made the clouds its garment,

and thick darkness its swaddling band,
¹⁰and prescribed bounds for it,
and set bars and doors,
¹¹and said, 'Thus far shall you come, and no farther,
and here shall your proud waves be stopped'?

¹²"Have you commanded the morning since your days began,
and caused the dawn to know its place,
¹³so that it might take hold of the skirts of the earth,
and the wicked be shaken out of it?
¹⁴It is changed like clay under the seal,
and it is dyed like a garment.
¹⁵Light is withheld from the wicked,
and their uplifted arm is broken.

¹⁶"Have you entered into the springs of the sea,
or walked in the recesses of the deep?
¹⁷Have the gates of death been revealed to you,
or have you seen the gates of deep darkness?
¹⁸Have you comprehended the expanse of the earth?
Declare, if you know all this.

¹⁹"Where is the way to the dwelling of light,
and where is the place of darkness,
²⁰that you may take it to its territory
and that you may discern the paths to its home?
²¹Surely you know, for you were born then,
and the number of your days is great!

²²"Have you entered the storehouses of the snow,
or have you seen the storehouses of the hail,
²³which I have reserved for the time of trouble,
for the day of battle and war?
²⁴What is the way to the place where the light is distributed,
or where the east wind is scattered upon the earth?

²⁵"Who has cut a channel for the torrents of rain,
and a way for the thunderbolt,

²⁶to bring rain on a land where no one lives,
  on the desert, which is empty of human life,
²⁷to satisfy the waste and desolate land,
  and to make the ground put forth grass?"

The book of Job is the tale of a "blameless and upright" man (1:1) who loses everything he has—livestock, family, and health—in a series of disasters. His suffering is so great that he wishes he had died at birth (3:11). He curses his creation and demands that God tell him why this has happened. Into Job's troubles comes a series of friends who only make things worse by trying to offer logical explanations for the mystery of innocent suffering. Venting his anger and despair, Job is tormented not only by his suffering but also by the silence of God.

At the end of the book, God finally answers Job in the midst of a great storm, manifesting God's powerful and mysterious presence in the midst of the wild energy of creation (verse 1). The whirlwind evokes Job's own stormy life, battered about by chaotic forces, as well as the wild freedom and deeply unsettling nature of God. The Lord challenges Job to prepare for a confrontation, to wrestle and struggle for a deeper understanding (verse 3). As Job has questioned the Lord, so now the Lord questions him. The cascading rhetorical questions of God's speech are a means of divine instruction, inviting both Job and the reader to reflect on the nature of God's relationship to creation.

Job's divine education is accomplished by overwhelming him with the magnificence of the created world. In wide-eyed, slack-jawed wonder, Job is confronted with the majesty of God as reflected in the vastness and incomprehensible beauty and energy of nature. Job had questioned whether God was really in control of the world, and here is the Lord's unmistakable response. God's sovereignty is presented in his creation of the earth (verses 4–7), the sea (verses 8–11), the heavens (verses 12–15), and the underworld (verses 16–18). The language of God is playful sarcasm: Where were you when I established the world's foundations? Surely you know how I formed the stars and contained the vast sea? You must certainly be old enough to remember and understand these things. God reminds Job that there are things that are simply beyond the limits of his understanding. Through repeated lessons from creation, God removes Job's focus from himself and broadens his horizon.

As the starting point of Job's new understanding, God asks Job to silently contemplate the created world. It is as if God brings Job on retreat: a quiet day in the forest, a day on the high seas, and a night gazing at the star-studded sky. As they did for Job, the wonders of God's creation are able to teach us the virtues of attentiveness, humility, and gratitude. They take the focus off of ourselves, and place it on the sovereign Creator of all.

Reflection and discussion

• When have I been overwhelmed by an awesome experience of the natural world?

• How does God shift Job's focus? What helps me take the focus away from my self-centered concerns?

• What parts of nature help me humbly recognize the limits of my own under-standing?

Prayer

Lord of Creation, you are the Creator and first cause of the earth, sky, and sea. Help me humbly recognize my place in your creation and be aware of the limits of my understanding. Help me be truly wise and humble as you teach me your ways.

"Do you know when the mountain goats give birth?
Do you observe the calving of the deer? Their young ones become strong,
they grow up in the open; they go forth, and do not return to them." Job 39:1, 4

Creation's Wild and Exuberant Freedom

JOB 38:28—39:18

[28] *"Has the rain a father,*
or who has begotten the drops of dew?
[29] *From whose womb did the ice come forth,*
and who has given birth to the hoarfrost of heaven?
[30] *The waters become hard like stone,*
and the face of the deep is frozen.

[31] *"Can you bind the chains of the Pleiades,*
or loose the cords of Orion?
[32] *Can you lead forth the Mazzaroth in their season,*
or can you guide the Bear with its children?
[33] *Do you know the ordinances of the heavens?*
Can you establish their rule on the earth?

[34] *"Can you lift up your voice to the clouds,*
so that a flood of waters may cover you?

³⁵*Can you send forth lightnings, so that they may go*
   and say to you, 'Here we are'?
³⁶*Who has put wisdom in the inward parts,*
   or given understanding to the mind?
³⁷*Who has the wisdom to number the clouds?*
   Or who can tilt the waterskins of the heavens,
³⁸*when the dust runs into a mass*
   and the clods cling together?

³⁹*"Can you hunt the prey for the lion,*
   or satisfy the appetite of the young lions,
⁴⁰*when they crouch in their dens,*
   or lie in wait in their covert?
⁴¹*Who provides for the raven its prey,*
   when its young ones cry to God,
   and wander about for lack of food?

39 ¹*"Do you know when the mountain goats give birth?*
   Do you observe the calving of the deer?
²*Can you number the months that they fulfill,*
   and do you know the time when they give birth,
³*when they crouch to give birth to their offspring,*
   and are delivered of their young?
⁴*Their young ones become strong, they grow up in the open;*
   they go forth, and do not return to them.

⁵*"Who has let the wild ass go free?*
   Who has loosed the bonds of the swift ass,
⁶*to which I have given the steppe for its home,*
   the salt land for its dwelling place?
⁷*It scorns the tumult of the city;*
   it does not hear the shouts of the driver.
⁸*It ranges the mountains as its pasture,*
   and it searches after every green thing.

⁹*"Is the wild ox willing to serve you?*
   Will it spend the night at your crib?

¹⁰*Can you tie it in the furrow with ropes,*
or will it harrow the valleys after you?
¹¹*Will you depend on it because its strength is great,*
and will you hand over your labor to it?
¹²*Do you have faith in it that it will return,*
and bring your grain to your threshing floor?

¹³*"The ostrich's wings flap wildly,*
though its pinions lack plumage.
¹⁴*For it leaves its eggs to the earth,*
and lets them be warmed on the ground,
¹⁵*forgetting that a foot may crush them,*
and that a wild animal may trample them.
¹⁶*It deals cruelly with its young, as if they were not its own;*
though its labor should be in vain, yet it has no fear;
¹⁷*because God has made it forget wisdom,*
and given it no share in understanding.
¹⁸*When it spreads its plumes aloft,*
it laughs at the horse and its rider.

God continues to offer Job a guided tour of creation in order to widen Job's perspective and show him that there is much that he can't understand. Whether it be the weather's rain, hail, dew, or frost (38:28–30), the movement of the constellations in the sky (38:31–33), or the wild freedom of the animal kingdom, the world responds to God's sovereignty in a way that is far beyond the limits of human wisdom. The world which seems dangerous and frighteningly out of control to Job is under the control of the God who is the loving cause of it all. Within this vastly broader perspective, Job can come to recover a sense of his own belonging and experience security within this rich panorama of God's creation.

Anyone who believes that the biblical literature teaches that God has created the non-human world merely for the benefit of people has not read the Bible carefully. In fact, this text and many others show that God delights in creatures which have no apparent human usefulness.

Job is just one of many creatures in the vastness of the created world. God watches over the goats and the deer in the mountains, counting the months of their pregnancy, and caring for them as they give birth, though they never encounter a human being (39:1–2). The lion, raven, goat, ass, and ox exist in a beautifully wild freedom, completely independent of human contact or purpose. They live in the mountains, the barren steppe, and the watery marshes, far from human settlement. Their freedom belongs to their nature and their instinctual wisdom enables them to survive and flourish.

God's reply to Job playfully derides him with surging questions and uses humor to open up Job's viewpoint. The silliness of the ostrich suggests that creation is a place of joy and laughter (39:13–18). As it wildly flaps its wings, it seems to be just for fun. Leaving its eggs on the ground, it acts irresponsibly by human standards of care and nurturing. Yet, while acting in a way devoid of any humanly recognizable understanding, somehow this foolish bird survives. In fact, when it spreads its plumes, it outruns the horse and its rider and laughs at them. The silly ostrich adds to the unique diversity of creation and demonstrates the divine humor of its Creator.

The diversity and magnitude of God's cosmic plan for creation baffles the mind of Job. The complexity and interdependence of both animate and inanimate creatures demonstrates God's provident attention to the minute details of the world. Job realizes he is completely ignorant of the behavior of these creatures, over which he has no influence or control. The scope of God's concern is not limited to the narrow confines of Job's world. God's questions underscore Job's creaturely limitations and emphasize that God's reign is far broader than the interests of human creation.

Reflection and discussion

• How does this vast panorama of creation offer Job a new sense a security and belonging?

• What is the purpose of this stream of questions that God asks Job?

• How do we know that creation's value exists independently of its usefulness to humans?

• What actions of my life today could demonstrate my belief in creation's goodness and value?

Prayer

Creator God, you give me unspeakable joy when I see creation's wonder and beauty. Help me increasingly recognize that the creatures of your world have value beyond their usefulness to me. May I always praise you for the vastness of your care for all of your creation.

"Is it by your wisdom that the hawk soars, and spreads its wings toward the south? Is it at your command that the eagle mounts up and makes its nest on high?" Job 39:26–27

Job Learns His Place in the World

JOB 39:19–40:5; 42:1–6

[19] *"Do you give the horse its might?*
Do you clothe its neck with mane?
[20] *Do you make it leap like the locust?*
Its majestic snorting is terrible.
[21] *It paws violently, exults mightily;*
it goes out to meet the weapons.
[22] *It laughs at fear, and is not dismayed;*
it does not turn back from the sword.
[23] *Upon it rattle the quiver,*
the flashing spear, and the javelin.
[24] *With fierceness and rage it swallows the ground;*
it cannot stand still at the sound of the trumpet.
[25] *When the trumpet sounds, it says 'Aha!'*
From a distance it smells the battle,
the thunder of the captains, and the shouting.

²⁶ *"Is it by your wisdom that the hawk soars,*
and spreads its wings toward the south?
²⁷ *Is it at your command that the eagle mounts up*
and makes its nest on high?
²⁸ *It lives on the rock and makes its home*
in the fastness of the rocky crag.
²⁹ *From there it spies the prey;*
its eyes see it from far away.
³⁰ *Its young ones suck up blood;*
and where the slain are, there it is."

40 ¹ *And the Lord said to Job:*
² *"Shall a faultfinder contend with the Almighty?*
Anyone who argues with God must respond."

³ *Then Job answered the Lord:*
⁴ *"See, I am of small account; what shall I answer you?*
I lay my hand on my mouth.
⁵ *I have spoken once, and I will not answer;*
twice, but will proceed no further."

42 ¹ *Then Job answered the Lord:*
² *"I know that you can do all things,*
and that no purpose of yours can be thwarted.
³ *'Who is this that hides counsel without knowledge?'*
Therefore I have uttered what I did not understand,
things too wonderful for me, which I did not know.
⁴ *'Hear, and I will speak;*
I will question you, and you declare to me.'
⁵ *I had heard of you by the hearing of the ear,*
but now my eye sees you;
⁶ *therefore I despise myself,*
and repent in dust and ashes."

In the midst of his suffering, Job had objected to the way God governs the world. But God, "the Almighty," has responded to Job, "the faultfinder" (40:2). Job now realizes that he must hand over his life to God more trustingly. He knows that his attempt to judge or control God based on his own expectations of what God should be like is foolish indeed. The magnitude of God's creation has humbled Job and enabled him to admit his human limitations. Job's new mind-set is one of submission before a reality far greater than he, and Job's response is humble silence (40:4–5).

Throughout this final section of the book of Job, one note resounds again and again and Job has heard it: the Lord is God and Job is not. With repentance Job admits his lack of understanding of the marvels of God's power. The dominion of God over creation is too wonderful for him to comprehend: "I have uttered what I did not understand, things too wonderful for me, which I did not know" (42:3). Job is now able to more clearly understand the limited scope of his own influence as a part of God's creation.

Transformed by the overwhelming presence of God manifested in the created world, Job can only stand in awe and wonder. God seems to take great delight in pointing out how utterly useless some parts of creation are to humans. Some things exist simply to display the splendor of God's act of creation. They confound and frustrate human wisdom, and they destroy our illusion of control. They make it clear that God, not humanity, is at the center of things. The scope of God's creative will reaches much farther than any human concern.

Because nature offers us a clearer sense of our human dependence and limitations, it teaches us to worship the Creator. In times of suffering and grief, there is deep solace in knowing there is a vast and wild world where only God is sovereign. When the human person no longer seeks to be in control, and a rightful place is left for the other wild and magnificent creatures of the world, the expanse of the natural world seems to be able to absorb some of the weight of human sorrow and pain. When Job is able to acknowledge this awesome quality of nature, he is able to better see his own place and role within the context of God's whole creation. With his new understanding, Job's fortune, family, and health are restored. He has been given a new awareness of God and he sees his own life with new perspective. Now, able to look to the future with greater trust and deeper confidence, Job lives to see better days than he had dreamed of.

This finale of the book of Job invites us to participate in God's raging creativity and to help create a world in which people and all creatures are able to live fully and flourish. Today, the awe which Job was able to experience in creation has unfortunately given way to human management and exploitation of nature. The insights of Job can challenge us to confront the ways in which our consumerist world prevents any part of God's creation from thriving. The magnificence of the world calls us to cast off our fears and anxiety, to live in confidence and trust, and to joyfully labor for justice on the earth for all its creatures.

Reflection and discussion

• How do the images of creation provided for Job help absorb the weight of his pain and grief? Has the wonder of nature ever helped relieve my suffering and loss?

• How does recognizing the beauty of the world impel me outward to work joyfully on behalf of the world's creatures?

Prayer

Sovereign Lord, you are the source of all the creative energy and beauty of the world. In my fears and pains, comfort me with the knowledge of my place in the vast splendor of your creation. Give me the desire to work joyfully on behalf of your creation.

I was daily his delight, rejoicing before him always,
rejoicing in his inhabited world and
delighting in the human race. Prov 8:30–31

Listen to God's Wisdom

PROVERBS 8:22–36

²² *The Lord created me at the beginning of his work,*
the first of his acts of long ago.
²³ *Ages ago I was set up,*
at the first, before the beginning of the earth.
²⁴ *When there were no depths I was brought forth,*
when there were no springs abounding with water.
²⁵ *Before the mountains had been shaped,*
before the hills, I was brought forth—
²⁶ *when he had not yet made earth and fields,*
or the world's first bits of soil.
²⁷ *When he established the heavens, I was there,*
when he drew a circle on the face of the deep,
²⁸ *when he made firm the skies above,*
when he established the fountains of the deep,
²⁹ *when he assigned to the sea its limit,*
so that the waters might not transgress his command,
when he marked out the foundations of the earth,
³⁰ *then I was beside him, like a master worker;*

47

and I was daily his delight,
  rejoicing before him always,
[31]rejoicing in his inhabited world
  and delighting in the human race.

[32]"And now, my children, listen to me:
  happy are those who keep my ways.
[33]Hear instruction and be wise,
  and do not neglect it.
[34]Happy is the one who listens to me,
  watching daily at my gates,
  waiting beside my doors.
[35]For whoever finds me finds life
  and obtains favor from the Lord;
[36]but those who miss me injure themselves;
  all who hate me love death."

Wisdom is that divine quality through which God created a world with meaning, order, and goodness. Humans can come to know wisdom through cultivating a contemplative understanding of the created world in all of its wonder. Through understanding wisdom, humanity will be able to recognize the presence of God within creation and appreciate God's love for the created world and his care for it. God desires that people come to know wisdom so that they can contribute to the created world in a way that is in harmony with the meaning, order, and goodness with which the world was created.

In this passage from Proverbs, wisdom is personified through a poetic description of wisdom's qualities in terms of a beautiful, wise, and good woman. By coming to know Woman Wisdom, God's people will understand both the nature of God and their own humanity and they will value their God-given role of caring for all that God loves.

The poet describes the origin of wisdom in order to help the reader understand wisdom's relationship to God and to creation. She is the offspring of the Creator, "created" at the beginning of God's work, the "first" of his creative actions (verse 22). Before the creation of the world, she was "set up" and "brought forth" by God so that she could share in God's creative work (verses 23–24). Since the "firstborn" in Israel's culture was the most valued, the one dedicated to God, so wisdom is described as the best and most treasured of all that came forth from God's creativity.

The verses then describe how wisdom was with God as God brought forth the elements of creation: the mountains and hills, the heavenly bodies, and the seas (verses 24–29). She was at the side of God "like a master worker" (verse 30). The image is that of an architect who designs and builds the cosmos, a collaborator in a creation that most clearly manifests God's wisdom. Wisdom designed the elements of the cosmos and is still active in the world. Wisdom is thus the link between the Creator and creation, the mediator between the invisible world of God and the inhabited earth. The work of creation is described as a joyful delight, a cause for enjoyment and rejoicing (verses 30–31). It is this divine "delight" in creation and this divine wisdom through which it is made that enables the created world to endure and flourish.

Since all that God has created has been made with wisdom, then humanity ought to continue God's creative activity with the aid of wisdom. Because everything in the world exists by wisdom, then it is by wisdom that the world is rightly used. Wisdom is fundamental to the whole creative process, giving to creation the direction, good structure, and stability which assures its continuation. Wisdom rules and contains the chaos which continually threatens to bring creation back to the disorder and meaninglessness from which it came. By following the ways of wisdom, human beings keep chaos at bay and continue the process of fashioning creation into an order that is good, beautiful, and meaningful.

In addition to being portrayed as a wise woman and a master worker, wisdom is also described as a teacher (verse 32–36). The divine wisdom used by God in creating and sustaining the world is offered to human beings. Those who hear her and listen to her instruction become wise. Those who find wisdom learn the purpose and direction of life. Those who embody the teachings of wisdom learn how to live well, to experience creation's life-sustaining power, and to care for themselves and for the world rather than abuse it. But those who reject the search for wisdom bring disarray to their own lives and disrupt the good order of creation.

Reflection and discussion

• Why is a contemplative approach to creation necessary for attaining wisdom? What do I learn when I reflect and meditate on the wonders of creation?

• What is the relationship between the Creator and Woman Wisdom? Why is it so important that people learn from her?

• Attaining wisdom was critical in the ancient world for learning how to live well. What happens when people today reject the search for wisdom?

Prayer

Holy Wisdom, you were with God at the beginning of creation and you continue to fill the world with beauty, goodness, order, and meaning. Help me learn from your instruction so that I may be truly wise and care for creation with the love of its Creator.

If through delight in the beauty of these things people assumed them to be gods, let them know how much better than these is their Lord, for the author of beauty created them. Wis 13:3

The Author of Created Beauty

WISDOM 13:1–9

¹*For all people who were ignorant of God were foolish by nature;*
and they were unable from the good things that are seen
    to know the one who exists,
nor did they recognize the artisan while paying heed to his works;
²*but they supposed that either fire or wind or swift air,*
or the circle of the stars, or turbulent water,
or the luminaries of heaven were the gods that rule the world.
³*If through delight in the beauty of these things people assumed them*
    to be gods,
let them know how much better than these is their Lord,
for the author of beauty created them.
⁴*And if people were amazed at their power and working,*
let them perceive from them
how much more powerful is the one who formed them.
⁵*For from the greatness and beauty of created things*
comes a corresponding perception of their Creator.

⁶Yet these people are little to be blamed,
for perhaps they go astray
while seeking God and desiring to find him.
⁷For while they live among his works, they keep searching,
and they trust in what they see,
    because the things that are seen are beautiful.
⁸Yet again, not even they are to be excused;
⁹for if they had the power to know so much
that they could investigate the world,
how did they fail to find sooner the Lord of these things?

The wisdom literature is filled with verses expressing amazement and wonder at the beauty of the natural world. But that admiration of the world is always accompanied by faith in the one who created such beauty. For the biblical writer, worshiping the Creator is the natural response to appreciating the wonders of the earth, sky, and sea.

The philosophical author reflects on the foolishness of those who admire the good things of the world but are unable to know God (verse 1). Seeing the goodness, diversity, order, and beauty of creation ought to lead a person to knowledge of their source, the Creator and cause of it all. The sage calls this first cause and primary source of all things "the one who is." This term for God is both the name by which God revealed himself to Moses (Exod 3:14) and also the term describing the deity in Greek philosophy. But though Greek thought was able to understand God as transcendent being, it did not proceed to describe God as Creator. Fortunately, God's revelation to the Israelites led to the understanding that "the one who is" is the Creator of all that exists, the transcendent deity on whom the universe is totally dependent. While marveling at the works of creation, they were able to recognize "the artisan," the personal Creator who made them all.

Human beings have a natural attraction to beauty. This innate longing for what is beautiful can be cultivated and refined by contemplative reflection on the experience of beauty. Much of the biblical literature is this kind of thoughtful reflection about the attractiveness of the world. Stars, sunrises, rainbows, mountains, trees, and flowers are praised for their beauty. The Song of Songs, for example, is a small anthology of the beauties of nature. Often, however, people in the ancient world made the mistake of worshiping the alluring creation rather than the Creator. They assumed the sun, moon, stars, fiery storm, or turbulent sea to be gods who ruled the world (verse 2). As the sage describes it, "Through delight in the beauty of these things people assumed them to be gods" (verse 3).

People today sometimes draw similar conclusions because of the attractive power of natural beauty. Various expressions of pantheism identify God with the world and the world with God. The biblical writers, however, always express the transcendence of God as distinct from the world of created reality, but at the same time insist that God can be known through observing the power, beauty, order, and goodness of the world. This sacramental view of the world insists that nature is not God, but the natural world points us to the existence of God: "From the greatness and beauty of created things comes a corresponding perception of their Creator" (verse 5).

Paul expressed this same understanding in his letter to the Romans: "Ever since the creation of the world [God's] eternal power and divine nature, invisible though they are, have been understood and seen through the things he has made" (Rom 1:20). Works of art bear the imprint of the mind and heart of the artist. Creation bears the imprint of "the author of beauty" (verse 3), and through its beauty humanity experiences something of its Creator's wisdom, power, and goodness.

Reflection and discussion

• Why is beauty so attractive to us? What does the title "author of beauty" tell me about God?

• How does reflecting on the world's beauty lead me to worship God?

• Why is it so tempting for people to worship a creature rather than the Creator?

• In what ways do I experience Paul's sacramental view of the world expressed in Romans 1:20?

Prayer

Author of Beauty, you are the source and cause of all that exists. Give me the insight to see your eternal power and creative love in the things you have made. As I reflect on the beauty you have made, lead me to worship you as the Creator and Lord of all.

Look at the rainbow, and praise him who made it;
it is exceedingly beautiful in its brightness. It encircles the sky
with its glorious arc; the hands of the Most High have stretched it out.

Sir 43:11–12

Praise and Exalt the Lord of Earth and Sky

SIRACH 43:9–26

⁹*The glory of the stars is the beauty of heaven,*
  a glittering array in the heights of the Lord.
¹⁰*On the orders of the Holy One they stand in their appointed places;*
  they never relax in their watches.
¹¹*Look at the rainbow, and praise him who made it;*
  it is exceedingly beautiful in its brightness.
¹²*It encircles the sky with its glorious arc;*
  the hands of the Most High have stretched it out.

¹³*By his command he sends the driving snow*
  and speeds the lightnings of his judgment.
¹⁴*Therefore the storehouses are opened,*
  and the clouds fly out like birds.
¹⁵*In his majesty he gives the clouds their strength,*
  and the hailstones are broken in pieces.

¹⁶*The voice of his thunder rebukes the earth;*
   when he appears, the mountains shake.
¹⁷*At his will the south wind blows;*
   so do the storm from the north and the whirlwind.
He scatters the snow like birds flying down,
   and its descent is like locusts alighting.
¹⁸*The eye is dazzled by the beauty of its whiteness,*
   and the mind is amazed as it falls.
¹⁹*He pours frost over the earth like salt,*
   and icicles form like pointed thorns.
²⁰*The cold north wind blows,*
   and ice freezes on the water;
it settles on every pool of water,
   and the water puts it on like a breastplate.
²¹*He consumes the mountains and burns up the wilderness,*
   and withers the tender grass like fire.
²²*A mist quickly heals all things;*
   the falling dew gives refreshment from the heat.
²³*By his plan he stilled the deep*
   and planted islands in it.
²⁴*Those who sail the sea tell of its dangers,*
   and we marvel at what we hear.
²⁵*In it are strange and marvelous creatures,*
   all kinds of living things, and huge sea-monsters.
²⁶*Because of him each of his messengers succeeds,*
   and by his word all things hold together.

If this wisdom sage were composing the book of Sirach today, perhaps he would substitute this series of word images with pages of photography: a star-studded night sky (verse 9), a rainbow across a rain-soaked landscape (verse 11), a gathering storm with lightning flashing across a dark-gray sky (verses 14–17), a snowy scene covered with a blanket of white (verses 17–18), crystallized frost and icicles hanging from trees around a frozen lake (verses 19–20), a misty morning covering a mountain with dew (verse 22), and a ship rolling on the waves of the sea (verse 24). The words of these verses stir the memories and imaginations of their hearers today just as powerfully as when they were read within the gatherings of ancient Israelites. This wondrous world which we inhabit is both a work of God and a revelation of God. The land, sky, and sea have been created by God, exist for God's pleasure and purpose, and demonstrate the marvelous goodness and the creative genius of their loving source.

There are two great "books" through which we come to know God: the book of God's word, revealed in Scripture, and the book of God's work, revealed in creation. Through each of these sources, humanity has the wonderful opportunity of coming to a relationship with God. In the works of creation, God's revelation is always and everywhere able to be seen. Though no one is capable of seeing God, we can know God's eternal power and divine nature through the wonders he has created.

In our worship our response to God's revelation must express the joy and exuberance of knowing God as the Creator, the sovereign source of all being. The ancient sages expressed this wonder and enjoyment which they experienced in God's mighty works. Today, when Christian worship becomes too introspective and faith becomes too personal and individualistic, then worship loses its joyful power to transform people. In authentic worship, God must be experienced as not only the Lord of heaven above but also the Maker of earth beneath. We must worship with all creation and experience creation in our praise. Only when people exalt the God of earth, sky, and sea and include creation in their worship, only then can worshipers experience that unspeakable joy with which we were made to worship our Creator God.

Reflection and discussion

• What scene of created beauty has recently given me joy? How did it lead me to praise God?

• Why are both God's word and God's work necessary sources for coming to know and understand God?

• In what ways can communal worship of God include elements of creation so that it becomes less individualistic and more expansive? How can we praise God as Creator of the earth as well as the Lord of heaven?

• How have poetry, painting, photography, or music given me a richer appreciation of the created world?

Prayer

Creator of the earth, sky, and sea, all the elements of the world naturally give you praise. Help me realize that you are the sovereign Lord of this wondrous world, and give me joy in worshiping you along with all your creatures.

SUGGESTIONS FOR FACILITATORS, GROUP SESSION 3

1. Welcome group members and ask if there are any announcements anyone would like to make.

2. You may want to pray this prayer as a group:

Lord of the earth, sky, and sea, the sages of ancient Israel marveled at the magnificence and power manifested in your works. Give me the insight to perceive your eternal power and creative love in the things you have made. The vast energy and beauty of nature displays your wise plan for the world which we are unable to comprehend. As we contemplate the books of your Scripture and the revelation of your world, teach us humility so that we may more deeply understand our place in the vast splendor of creation.

3. Ask one or both of the following questions:
   - Which image from the lessons this week stands out most memorably to you?
   - What is the most important lesson you learned through your study this week?

4. Discuss lessons 7 through 12. Choose one or more of the questions for reflection and discussion from each lesson to discuss as a group. You may want to ask group members which question was most challenging or helpful to them as you review each lesson.

5. Remember that there are no definitive answers for these discussion questions. The insights of group members will add to the understanding of all. None of these questions require an expert.

6. After talking about each lesson, instruct group members to complete lessons 13 through 18 on their own during the six days before the next group meeting. They should write out their own answers to the questions as preparation for next week's group discussion.

7. Ask the group if anyone is having any particular problems with the Bible study during the week. You may want to share advice and encouragement within the group.

8. Conclude by praying aloud together the prayer at the end of one of the lessons discussed. You may add to the prayer based on the sharing that has occurred in the group.

God made the wild animals of the earth of every kind,
and the cattle of every kind, and everything that creeps upon
the ground of every kind. **And God saw that it was good.** Gen 1:25

All Creatures at Home on the Earth

GENESIS 1:1–25 *¹In the beginning when God created the heavens and the earth, ²the earth was a formless void and darkness covered the face of the deep, while a wind from God swept over the face of the waters. ³Then God said, "Let there be light"; and there was light. ⁴And God saw that the light was good; and God separated the light from the darkness. ⁵God called the light Day, and the darkness he called Night. And there was evening and there was morning, the first day.*

⁶And God said, "Let there be a dome in the midst of the waters, and let it separate the waters from the waters." ⁷So God made the dome and separated the waters that were under the dome from the waters that were above the dome. And it was so. ⁸God called the dome Sky. And there was evening and there was morning, the second day.

⁹And God said, "Let the waters under the sky be gathered together into one place, and let the dry land appear." And it was so. ¹⁰God called the dry land Earth, and the waters that were gathered together he called Seas. And God saw that it was good. ¹¹Then God said, "Let the earth put forth vegetation: plants yielding seed, and fruit trees of every kind on earth that bear fruit with the seed in it." And it was so. ¹²The earth brought forth vegetation: plants yielding seed of every kind, and trees of every kind bearing fruit with the seed in it. And God saw that it was good. ¹³*And there was evening and there was morning, the third day.*

¹⁴*And God said, "Let there be lights in the dome of the sky to separate the day from the night; and let them be for signs and for seasons and for days and years,* ¹⁵*and let them be lights in the dome of the sky to give light upon the earth." And it was so.* ¹⁶*God made the two great lights—the greater light to rule the day and the lesser light to rule the night—and the stars.* ¹⁷*God set them in the dome of the sky to give light upon the earth,* ¹⁸*to rule over the day and over the night, and to separate the light from the darkness. And God saw that it was good.* ¹⁹*And there was evening and there was morning, the fourth day.*

²⁰*And God said, "Let the waters bring forth swarms of living creatures, and let birds fly above the earth across the dome of the sky."* ²¹*So God created the great sea monsters and every living creature that moves, of every kind, with which the waters swarm, and every winged bird of every kind. And God saw that it was good.* ²²*God blessed them, saying, "Be fruitful and multiply and fill the waters in the seas, and let birds multiply on the earth."* ²³*And there was evening and there was morning, the fifth day.*

²⁴*And God said, "Let the earth bring forth living creatures of every kind: cattle and creeping things and wild animals of the earth of every kind." And it was so.* ²⁵*God made the wild animals of the earth of every kind, and the cattle of every kind, and everything that creeps upon the ground of every kind. And God saw that it was good.*

This creation account of Israel's literature does not answer the question, "How was the world made?" but rather the more important question, "Why was the world made?" Far from being a scientific report of how things came to be, the description of God's creation uses poetic language to express the meaning and purpose of the world and all its creatures. Its form suggests that it was written to be proclaimed in worship by the ancient Israelites. As liturgical poetry, it invites the congregation to proclaim and celebrate the world as God intended it to be. Its message is the good news that Creator and creation are bound together in a relationship that is trustworthy while at the same time delicate.

Before God began the process of creation, the earth was a "formless void" and darkness covered the primordial waters (verse 2). There was nothing but gloom, chaos, and emptiness. But God's creative will brought light into the darkness, form from the chaos, and living creatures into the void. This account presents the process of creation in six frames called days. Each frame follows a fixed pattern that begins with "and God said" and finishes with "and there was evening and there was morning...." The account's comprehensiveness indicates that everything in heaven and earth owes its existence to the sovereign will of God.

The ordering of each of the first three days corresponds to what is created on days four through six. On day one God created the light and separated it from the darkness. On the fourth day, God made the light-giving bodies that govern the day and the night—the sun, moon, and stars. On day two God separated the massive body of water into two parts with a great dome. The waters placed above the expanse house the rain, hail, and snow, and the waters below feed the seas, rivers, and springs. On the fifth day, God filled the space he had created—the sky and the seas—with the winged birds of every kind and the variety of living creatures that swarm the waters. On day three God separated the dry land from the seas, and he called forth the plants and trees to grow upon the earth. On the sixth day, God filled the earth with wild and domestic animals and all kinds of living creatures.

Though its ancient cosmology is quite different from our scientific understanding of the universe today, this creation account expresses the beauty and purpose of the world in a wonderful way. It leads worshipers to praise God as the wise, all-powerful Creator and establishes a clear distinction between the transcendent Creator and the diverse elements of his creation. Each member of creation has its own purpose and responsibility: the light-giving bodies in the heavens establish times and seasons; the living creatures must be fruitful and multiply. Most significantly, God evaluates each element of creation and pronounces it "good" (verses 4, 10, 12, 18, 21, 25). Each creature contributes to the well-being of the created order and each is beautiful and pleasing to God.

This orderly expression of God's creative will disputes any attempt to focus on humanity as the sole purpose of creation. God's first blessing is not for humankind, but for all the creatures of the sky and seas (verse 22). God is the Lord of all creation and has his own relationship with the individual creatures independent of humanity. God values each element in creation as "good," and each creature has its own purpose and role within the wondrous work of God.

Reflection and discussion

• Why is this creation account most appropriately proclaimed in liturgical worship? How does it inspire me with reverence for God's creation?

• Why would the writer use the framework of Israel's traditional week to express God's creative power in this account?

• What does God's declaration that each element of creation is "good" tell me about the value of the natural world?

Prayer

Creator of the heavens and the earth, it is your will to create a wondrous and beautiful diversity within the world. Help me see the world as an intricate tapestry that bears witness to your divine creativity. May I always praise you for your goodness reflected in each element of creation.

"To every beast of the earth, and to every bird of the air,
and to everything that creeps on the earth, everything that has the breath
of life, I have given every green plant for food." Gen 1:30

Everything God Makes Is Very Good

GENESIS 1:26—2:3 ²⁶ *Then God said, "Let us make humankind in our image, according to our likeness; and let them have dominion over the fish of the sea, and over the birds of the air, and over the cattle, and over all the wild animals of the earth, and over every creeping thing that creeps upon the earth."*
²⁷ *So God created humankind in his image,*
in the image of God he created them;
male and female he created them.
²⁸ *God blessed them, and God said to them, "Be fruitful and multiply, and fill the earth and subdue it; and have dominion over the fish of the sea and over the birds of the air and over every living thing that moves upon the earth." ²⁹ God said, "See, I have given you every plant yielding seed that is upon the face of all the earth, and every tree with seed in its fruit; you shall have them for food. ³⁰ And to every beast of the earth, and to every bird of the air, and to everything that creeps on the earth, everything that has the breath of life, I have given every green plant for food." And it was so. ³¹ God saw everything that he had made, and indeed, it was very good. And there was evening and there was morning, the sixth day.*

2 ¹*Thus the heavens and the earth were finished, and all their multitude.* ²*And on the seventh day God finished the work that he had done, and he rested on the seventh day from all the work that he had done.* ³*So God blessed the seventh day and hallowed it, because on it God rested from all the work that he had done in creation.*

Though each creature has its own purpose in God's plan, and God delights in all of his creation, it is clear from this liturgical poetry that there is something unique and special about humanity. The human creature is created on the same day as the other animals of the earth, suggesting that they have much in common, but at the same time, the text proclaims that humankind is made in God's "image" and "likeness" (verse 26). God has a unique, intimate relationship with his human creatures. God speaks directly only to them (verses 28–29). Clearly, this final creation is the climax of God's work, offering to the human creature a unique purpose and responsibility within the world as God intended it to be.

The proclamation that humankind is made in the image and likeness of God indicates, on the one hand, that man and woman are not divine, but, on the other hand, that they are a unique reflection of God in the world. In the cultures of the ancient Near East, the king was described as the image of God, meaning that the monarch was God's representative on earth. Here the man and the woman are the royal representatives of God in the world. God bestows upon them "dominion" over the rest of the natural world (verse 26). This royal terminology suggests that humanity is given authority and responsibility for the well-being and enhancement of creation. The task of "dominion" has nothing to do with domination, exploitation, or abuse. The role of the human person is to ensure that the work of God becomes fully the creation willed by its Creator.

God's command that the man and woman "subdue" the earth and "have dominion" over its creatures instructs them to govern the earth in a way that cares for its creatures with wisdom (verse 28). Humans must rule the earth as God rules creation. This governance means that humans must promote the well-being of earth's creatures and protect them from danger, just as a monarch fosters the welfare of the kingdom's citizens. Though human beings have often used these texts to justify their own greedy exploitation of creation, the biblical context of these verses condemns pollution of the earth, sea, and sky, deforestation and species extinction, and other abuses of living creatures and their natural habitat. Human beings are accountable to God as his royal stewards of the earth, and refusal to govern wisely and care for the kingdom is a sin against the world's Creator.

At the end of this liturgical proclamation of God's creation, God rejoiced in his work and declared it "very good" (verse 31). God then rested from his work and blessed and hallowed the seventh day (2:2–3). As the great artist of the universe, God not only delights in the process of creation but also in accomplishing the beautiful masterpiece. The Sabbath day becomes the time for God's stewards to appreciate and rejoice in God's creation. The necessity of rest is written into God's creation. Space for leisure, for developing relationships with others, for worshiping God, and for enjoying the created world is an essential part of human life. Those who learn to make the seventh day holy will enjoy God's blessings and savor the gift of life.

Reflection and discussion

• What are the privileges and responsibilities involved in being made in the image of God?

• What indicates that human "dominion" over creation has nothing to do with "domination" of earth's creatures?

• What does the image of the wise monarch tell us about man and woman's responsibility for creation?

• In what ways have humans abused the privilege of representing God in their rule over creation?

• Do I have an appreciation of the world as "very good"? How could I deepen my love for the created world by contemplating its goodness in God's eyes?

Prayer

Wise Creator, you made man and woman in your image and gave us responsibility as stewards of your world. May we always rule the earth as you rule creation, always aware of your love for creation's diversity, beauty, and goodness.

The Lord God took the man and put him in the garden of Eden to till it and keep it. Gen 2:15

Called to Care for the Earth

GENESIS 2:4–25 ⁴*These are the generations of the heavens and the earth when they were created.*

In the day that the Lord God made the earth and the heavens, ⁵*when no plant of the field was yet in the earth and no herb of the field had yet sprung up—for the Lord God had not caused it to rain upon the earth, and there was no one to till the ground;* ⁶*but a stream would rise from the earth, and water the whole face of the ground—* ⁷*then the Lord God formed man from the dust of the ground, and breathed into his nostrils the breath of life; and the man became a living being.* ⁸*And the Lord God planted a garden in Eden, in the east; and there he put the man whom he had formed.* ⁹*Out of the ground the Lord God made to grow every tree that is pleasant to the sight and good for food, the tree of life also in the midst of the garden, and the tree of the knowledge of good and evil.*

¹⁰*A river flows out of Eden to water the garden, and from there it divides and becomes four branches.* ¹¹*The name of the first is Pishon; it is the one that flows around the whole land of Havilah, where there is gold;* ¹²*and the gold of that land is good; bdellium and onyx stone are there.* ¹³*The name of the second river is Gihon; it is the one that flows around the whole land of Cush.* ¹⁴*The name of the third river is Tigris, which flows east of Assyria. And the fourth river is the Euphrates.*

¹⁵ *The Lord God took the man and put him in the garden of Eden to till it and keep it.* ¹⁶ *And the Lord God commanded the man, "You may freely eat of every tree of the garden;* ¹⁷ *but of the tree of the knowledge of good and evil you shall not eat, for in the day that you eat of it you shall die."*
    ¹⁸ *Then the Lord God said, "It is not good that the man should be alone; I will make him a helper as his partner."* ¹⁹ *So out of the ground the Lord God formed every animal of the field and every bird of the air, and brought them to the man to see what he would call them; and whatever the man called every living crea-ture, that was its name.* ²⁰ *The man gave names to all cattle, and to the birds of the air, and to every animal of the field; but for the man there was not found a helper as his partner.* ²¹ *So the Lord God caused a deep sleep to fall upon the man, and he slept; then he took one of his ribs and closed up its place with flesh.* ²² *And the rib that the Lord God had taken from the man he made into a woman and brought her to the man.* ²³ *Then the man said,*

"This at last is bone of my bones
    and flesh of my flesh;
this one shall be called Woman,
    for out of Man this one was taken."
²⁴ *Therefore a man leaves his father and his mother and clings to his wife, and they become one flesh.* ²⁵ *And the man and his wife were both naked, and were not ashamed.*

This account of the garden in Genesis 2 shifts the focus from the whole creation to the responsibilities of human beings within creation. It is less liturgical and more colorful and story-like, probably a much older narrative than Genesis 1. The God who is the Creator of the heavens and the earth is now revealed as a loving provider. The one who offers the gift of life provides many other gifts to humanity.

God created the human being as part of the same creative process as the rest of earth's creatures: "God formed man from the dust of the ground, and breathed into his nostrils the breath of life" (verse 7). God formed the human (the *adam*, in Hebrew) from the ground (the *adamah*, in Hebrew). As the first creation account stressed the continuity between human beings and the rest of creation by describing the creation of animals and humans on the same day, this narrative describes the human being as created from the same ground as the other living creatures (verse 19). Today, we know that our continuity with the rest of creation is demonstrated by the fact that we share much in terms of biochemistry, behavior patterns, and genetic origins with the other animals.

This generous God then planted a garden in which he placed the human being whom he had formed (verse 8). The environment in which God placed his human being is abundant in its provision. Not only does this world provide for the everyday needs of the human, but it is wonderful in its beauty and diversity. It contains an abundance of trees that are both pleasant to view and good for food, shade, and shelter for the creatures (verse 9). The garden is watered by a river that divides into four branches (verse 10), and the mention of gold, bdellium, and onyx indicates a richness of natural resources (verse 12). This bountiful God not only offers gifts in abundance, but also infuses the garden with his presence and continually offers care and companionship.

With this gift of the garden comes the responsibility to maintain its beauty and its fruitfulness. God put the human being in the garden "to till it and keep it" (verse 15). The Hebrew word for "to till" is frequently translated "to serve" in other places in the Bible. To cultivate the earth is a form of service to God. The Hebrew word for "to keep" suggests the privilege of taking care of the garden and guarding it from harm. In this human care for the earthly environment, we see God's desired relationship between humanity and our earthly habitat. As custodians of God's gift, we must prudently conserve its riches and prevent its desecration and exploitation.

In striking contrast to the frequent description of creation as "good," God declared that it is "not good" for a person to be alone (verse 18). When God creates the woman from the flesh of the representative first human (the *adam*), the pair is called man (*'ish*, in Hebrew) and woman (*'ishah*). To call the woman a "helper" to the man does not imply a subordinate place, especially since God is frequently referred to as a helper to his people. The text describes, rather, the mutual support and companionship offered by man and woman to each other. As the same flesh and bone (verse 23), man and woman are equal in value, though wonderfully diverse in gender. Bonded in companionship and enriched by their sexual differences, they overcome their loneliness and experience fulfillment. Their nakedness expresses the mutual trust and respect that united man and woman and their harmonious relationship with the other creatures of the earth (verse 25).

Reflection and discussion

• What is the significance of the fact that the human being is formed from the same ground as the other living beings?

• What are the gifts and responsibilities God gives to the human species in the garden?

• How is this ideal image of the relationship between humanity and creation different from the actual experience of today's world?

Prayer

Generous Creator, out of your loving care for humanity you have given us the abundant gifts of the natural world. Give us the creativity and courage to take care of the earth and guard it from harm.

They heard the sound of the Lord God walking in the garden at the time of the evening breeze, and the man and his wife hid themselves from the presence of the Lord God among the trees of the garden. Gen 3:8

A World of Broken Bonds

GENESIS 3:1–13 ¹*Now the serpent was more crafty than any other wild animal that the Lord God had made. He said to the woman, "Did God say, 'You shall not eat from any tree in the garden'?" ²The woman said to the serpent, "We may eat of the fruit of the trees in the garden; ³but God said, 'You shall not eat of the fruit of the tree that is in the middle of the garden, nor shall you touch it, or you shall die.'" ⁴But the serpent said to the woman, "You will not die; ⁵for God knows that when you eat of it your eyes will be opened, and you will be like God, knowing good and evil." ⁶So when the woman saw that the tree was good for food, and that it was a delight to the eyes, and that the tree was to be desired to make one wise, she took of its fruit and ate; and she also gave some to her husband, who was with her, and he ate. ⁷Then the eyes of both were opened, and they knew that they were naked; and they sewed fig leaves together and made loincloths for themselves.*

⁸They heard the sound of the Lord God walking in the garden at the time of the evening breeze, and the man and his wife hid themselves from the presence of the Lord God among the trees of the garden. ⁹But the Lord God called to the man, and said to him, "Where are you?" ¹⁰He said, "I heard the sound of you in the garden, and I was afraid, because I was naked; and I hid myself." ¹¹He said, "Who told you that you were naked? Have you eaten from the tree of which I commanded you not to eat?" ¹²The man said, "The woman whom you gave to be with

72

me, she gave me fruit from the tree, and I ate." [13] *Then the Lord God said to the woman, "What is this that you have done?" The woman said, "The serpent tricked me, and I ate."*

The narrative of the garden conveys the message that man and woman are to live in God's world, along with God's other creatures, on God's terms. The beautiful and fruitful garden is God's gracious gift, a blessing which must be cared for and protected. Within the garden, the human creatures are given freedom, symbolized by God's permission to "freely eat of every tree of the garden" (2:16). Within this broad range of choices, they are given only one prohibition: "of the tree of the knowledge of good and evil you shall not eat, for in the day that you eat of it you shall die" (2:17). The forbidden fruit is the pursuit of knowledge without reference to God. Eating the fruit of this tree would give the illusion of self-sufficiency and independence from God, an inappropriate condition for a creature made from the ground.

Into this luscious garden crawls the serpent, the symbol of that which opposes God (verse 1). Through gentle seduction, the serpent misrepresents what God has said. The Creator who provides such wondrous beauty and abundant freedom is now presented as one who wants to restrict rather than give. In their act of rebellion, the man and woman reject their Creator and seek to become their own provider and lord. In their desire for autonomy, they deny that they are creatures bestowed with good and abundant gifts from their Creator.

The story illustrates how self-defeating and destructive it is to rebel against the natural order established by God. Man and woman's transgression against the boundaries set up by God disrupts their relationship with God, with themselves, and with creation itself. The harmony which God established in the garden becomes distorted. The mutual trust between man and woman becomes dominated by shame (verse 7). The God who walks in the garden with his creatures is now feared (verse 8). The trees that were so pleasant to the sight and good for food (2:9) now become a hiding place for the man and woman to avoid their Creator. The human creatures whom God made stewards and gave responsibility over the garden now pathetically blame one another and refuse to take responsibility (verse 12–13).

This is the story of human rejection of the Creator and all he has provided. The rebellion depicted is not simply the first sin; it is all human sin. As we listen to the story we realize that our sin, too, has cosmic dimensions and is an attack on creation. In the garden, God provided life, beauty, abundance, freedom, harmonious relationships, meaningful work, and leisure. Now humanity no longer walks with God in the garden and no longer accepts its responsibility to care for and protect the garden. God's original will for creation is distorted because its chief steward is no longer in harmony with God.

Reflection and discussion

• In what way does the story of man and woman in the garden express the ongoing human relationship with God?

• In what way does human transgression of boundaries established by the Creator disrupt our harmony with creation?

Prayer

Lord God, you desire to walk with us in the garden and share intimately in our lives. When we transgress the boundaries of your creation and rebel against your natural law, we distort your desire for creation. Teach me to live in the harmony which you have established for us.

Of the birds according to their kinds, and of the animals according to their kinds, of every creeping thing of the ground according to its kind, two of every kind shall come in to you, to keep them alive. Gen 6:20

Noah Called to Preserve the Species

GENESIS 6:11–22 ¹¹*Now the earth was corrupt in God's sight, and the earth was filled with violence.* ¹²*And God saw that the earth was corrupt; for all flesh had corrupted its ways upon the earth.*

¹³*And God said to Noah, "I have determined to make an end of all flesh, for the earth is filled with violence because of them; now I am going to destroy them along with the earth.* ¹⁴*Make yourself an ark of cypress wood; make rooms in the ark, and cover it inside and out with pitch.* ¹⁵*This is how you are to make it: the length of the ark three hundred cubits, its width fifty cubits, and its height thirty cubits.* ¹⁶*Make a roof for the ark, and finish it to a cubit above; and put the door of the ark in its side; make it with lower, second, and third decks.* ¹⁷*For my part, I am going to bring a flood of waters on the earth, to destroy from under heaven all flesh in which is the breath of life; everything that is on the earth shall die.* ¹⁸*But I will establish my covenant with you; and you shall come into the ark, you, your sons, your wife, and your sons' wives with you.* ¹⁹*And of every living thing, of all flesh, you shall bring two of every kind into the ark, to keep them alive with you; they shall be male and female.* ²⁰*Of the birds according to their kinds, and of*

the animals according to their kinds, of every creeping thing of the ground according to its kind, two of every kind shall come in to you, to keep them alive. ²¹Also take with you every kind of food that is eaten, and store it up; and it shall serve as food for you and for them."

²²Noah did this; he did all that God commanded him.

It is unfortunate that the account of Noah and the flood is generally regarded as a children's story, because it provides all responsible adults with a way to reflect on the cost of destructive human choices and the passionate care of God for creation. The narrative begins with the pending destruction of the earth due to the corruption and violence of its human inhabitants (verse 11–12). God realizes that something is deeply amiss with his human creation, so much so that God's purposes for creation have no prospect of fulfillment. God's human creatures have refused to live in the created world on God's terms, failing to exercise their responsibility to care for the world and to live in the harmony God desires. When God realizes that his beloved creation is in such danger, "the Lord was sorry that he had made humankind on the earth, and it grieved him to his heart" (verse 6). This is not an enraged judge, but a heartbroken parent. When God realizes that the human heart is evil and corrupt, God resolves to begin again, so uncompromisingly serious is God's purpose for creation.

The story of the flood, so common in the ancient literature of many cultures, is not the prime focus, but only a dramatic setting for the spotlight on the grieving, passionate, and determined heart of God for creation. God determines that he will not allow the corruption of humankind to sway him from his dream for a harmonious creation. So, in the righteous Noah, God envisions an alternative possibility for the world. Noah is the fully responsive human being, who accepts his creatureliness and responds to God's creative will. God instructs him to build the ark in order to save a remnant of his creation as the foundation for a renewed world.

The flooding waters represent the chaos that ruled before God formed the world (Gen 1:2). The refusal of man and woman to live on God's terms with God's other creatures had its effects on the natural world and reversed the ordered harmony of God's creation. The floods overturn God's orderly separation of the waters on creation's second day (Gen 1:6–7) and inundate the earth. But, obeying God's desires, Noah built the ark, not only to safeguard his own family, but to preserve creation. He carefully saved two of every living thing, a male and female of every species of birds, animals, creeping reptiles, and insects (verses 19–20). As the human being who responded to God's creative will, Noah wasted no time and spared no expense in building the ark when God's creatures were threatened with extinction.

Reflection and discussion

• What does the flood narrative tell me about the character and heart of God?

• How is the story of Noah and the flood a reflective story for responsible adults? In what way can contemporary humans model Noah's concern to preserve God's beloved creation?

Prayer

Passionate Creator, your heart grieves when you see destruction and violence within your creation. Make me a person who sees the world with your eyes and give me a heart that cares about the earth. Help me always seek to preserve the variety, abundance, and fertility of your creation.

I am establishing my covenant with you and your descendants after you,
and with every living creature that is with you, the birds,
the domestic animals, and every animal of the earth with you,
as many as came out of the ark. Gen 9:9–10

God's Covenant with All Creation

GENESIS 9:1–17 ¹*God blessed Noah and his sons, and said to them, "Be fruitful and multiply, and fill the earth. ²The fear and dread of you shall rest on every animal of the earth, and on every bird of the air, on everything that creeps on the ground, and on all the fish of the sea; into your hand they are delivered. ³Every moving thing that lives shall be food for you; and just as I gave you the green plants, I give you everything. ⁴Only, you shall not eat flesh with its life, that is, its blood. ⁵For your own lifeblood I will surely require a reckoning: from every animal I will require it and from human beings, each one for the blood of another, I will require a reckoning for human life.*

⁶*Whoever sheds the blood of a human,*
by a human shall that person's blood be shed;
for in his own image
God made humankind.
⁷*And you, be fruitful and multiply, abound on the earth and multiply in it."*

⁸*Then God said to Noah and to his sons with him, ⁹"As for me, I am establishing my covenant with you and your descendants after you, ¹⁰and with every liv-*

ing creature that is with you, the birds, the domestic animals, and every animal of the earth with you, as many as came out of the ark. ¹¹I establish my covenant with you, that never again shall all flesh be cut off by the waters of a flood, and never again shall there be a flood to destroy the earth." ¹²God said, "This is the sign of the covenant that I make between me and you and every living creature that is with you, for all future generations: ¹³I have set my bow in the clouds, and it shall be a sign of the covenant between me and the earth. ¹⁴When I bring clouds over the earth and the bow is seen in the clouds, ¹⁵I will remember my covenant that is between me and you and every living creature of all flesh; and the waters shall never again become a flood to destroy all flesh. ¹⁶When the bow is in the clouds, I will see it and remember the everlasting covenant between God and every living creature of all flesh that is on the earth." ¹⁷God said to Noah, "This is the sign of the covenant that I have established between me and all flesh that is on the earth."

The flooding waters subside; life begins again; there is new hope for creation. All the living creatures on the ark are released so they may thrive and proliferate on the earth. The blessing God gave to humankind in the original creation is restated for Noah and his family: "Be fruitful and multiply, and fill the earth" (verses 1, 7; see 1:28). The noble call to be God's representatives on earth is reaffirmed: "In his own image God made humankind" (verse 6; see 1:27). This renewed humanity is entrusted again with responsible rule over the other creatures of the earth. Yet, God's call to stewardship must now be lived in the new context of a sin-laden world.

The relationship between human beings and the natural world has been negatively affected. Now humans are permitted to eat the meat of animals, so long as their blood is not consumed (verse 4). But, as might be expected, the beasts, birds, and fish will live in "fear and dread" of the human creatures whose food will be provided at the expense of their lives (verses 2–3). The harmony of God's original desire for creation can no longer be assumed, and laws and structures of justice that limit the effects of human greed and destructiveness must be put in place. Penalties for murder and violence against human life must be particularly rigorous (verses 5–6). Economic incentives and punishments will be necessary to protect God's creation from the harmful results of self-centered living within the world.

Despite this fragile relationship between humans and other living creatures, God renews his relationship with the world and expresses an unending pledge to his creation. The covenant God establishes is an everlasting bond with humanity and with every living creature that came out of the ark (verses 9–10). As fellow-creatures, humanity and all living things are partners in the same covenant. God promises that "never again" will the floods destroy the earth (verse 11), making an irreversible commitment to stand for and with creation. This committed compassion of God for all the creatures of the earth makes new life possible and offers undying hope for the future.

God designates the rainbow as the sign of the covenant between God and the earth (verses 12–13). It is a reminder, both for God and for the creatures of the world, of God's solemn vow to care for creation, even in the midst of the consequences of human sin. This is God's unconditional "yes" to all life, a divine affirmation that can never be shattered, either by catastrophes throughout the course of history or by the corruption and destructive powers of humankind. This bond between God and the earth is unending and universal in the widest sense imaginable: "the everlasting covenant between God and every living creature of all flesh that is upon the earth" (verse 16). Since God is so committed to us and to his creation, we can trust that God's purposes for the world will be fulfilled.

Reflection and discussion

• How does God demonstrate his trust in humankind despite our destructive greed?

• Why are social structures, laws, penalties, and incentives necessary to protect God's creation?

• In what sense can this creation covenant be called an ecological covenant between God and the earth?

• Why is the rainbow such a wondrous sign of God's commitment to creation? What comes to mind when I gaze upon a rainbow?

Prayer

Lord God of all creation, you have bonded yourself in covenant with all the creatures of the earth. Give me passion to care for your world and vision to look upon the beauty you have created. When I see the rainbow in the clouds, help me trust in your undying commitment to the world and give me hope in all that you have promised.

SUGGESTIONS FOR FACILITATORS, GROUP SESSION 4

1. Welcome group members and ask if anyone has any questions, announcements, or requests.

2. You may want to pray this prayer as a group:

Compassionate Creator, you have made the world with all of its diverse wonders and pronounced it "very good." All the creatures of the earth form an intricate tapestry which bears witness to your divine creativity. You have placed us in the midst of the world and charged us to care for creation and guard its variety, fertility, and abundance. May the rainbow always remind us of your eternal covenant with every living creature and of our responsibility to reflect your image in all creation.

3. Ask one or both of the following questions:
   • What is the most difficult part of this study for you?
   • What insight stands out to you from the lessons this week?

4. Discuss lessons 13 through 18. Choose one or more of the questions for reflection and discussion from each lesson to discuss as a group. You may want to ask group members which question was most challenging or helpful to them as you review each lesson.

5. Keep the discussion moving, but allow time for the questions that provoke the most discussion. Encourage the group members to use "I" language in their responses.

6. After talking over each lesson, instruct group members to complete lessons 19 through 24 on their own during the six days before the next group meeting. They should write out their own answers to the questions as preparation for next week's session.

7. Ask the group what encouragement they need for the coming week. Ask the members to pray for the needs of one another during the week.

8. Conclude by praying aloud together the prayer at the end of one of the lessons discussed. You may choose to conclude the prayer by asking members to pray aloud any requests they may have.

The seventh year there shall be a sabbath of complete rest for the land,
a sabbath for the Lord: you shall not sow your field
or prune your vineyard. Lev 25:4

A Sabbath for the Creatures and the Land

EXODUS 20:8–11 ⁸*Remember the sabbath day, and keep it holy.* ⁹*Six days you shall labor and do all your work.* ¹⁰*But the seventh day is a sabbath to the Lord your God; you shall not do any work—you, your son or your daughter, your male or female slave, your livestock, or the alien resident in your towns.* ¹¹*For in six days the Lord made heaven and earth, the sea, and all that is in them, but rested the seventh day; therefore the Lord blessed the sabbath day and consecrated it.*

LEVITICUS 25:1–7 ¹*The Lord spoke to Moses on Mount Sinai, saying:* ²*Speak to the people of Israel and say to them: When you enter the land that I am giving you, the land shall observe a sabbath for the Lord.* ³*Six years you shall sow your field, and six years you shall prune your vineyard, and gather in their yield;* ⁴*but in the seventh year there shall be a sabbath of complete rest for the land, a sabbath for the Lord: you shall not sow your field or prune your vineyard.* ⁵*You shall not reap the aftergrowth of your harvest or gather the grapes of your unpruned vine: it shall be a year of complete rest for the land.* ⁶*You may eat what the land yields during its sabbath—you, your male and female slaves, your hired and your bound laborers who live with you;* ⁷*for your livestock also, and for the wild animals in your land all its yield shall be for food.*

Keeping the Sabbath has long been Israel's most important requirement for honoring God's covenant. It is the longest of the Ten Commandments given to Moses and arguably the one which offers the motivation for the others. The weekly Sabbath offers people a way of living which honors the natural rhythm of work and rest, providing a regular release from the tyranny of unrelenting labor. But the Sabbath is more than a holiday to rest up for another week of work. The Israelites are commanded to keep the Sabbath holy (Exod 20:8). In Hebrew, "holy" means withdrawn from common use and reserved for a special purpose associated with God.

Full of ecological wisdom, the Sabbath legislation is designed for all, especially those who might not easily find rest: men and women, landowners and slaves, Israelites and foreigners, humans and even livestock (Exod 20:10). The divisions and distinctions that human striving have erected are broken down on the Sabbath, and humans and animals find peace on God's day of rest. As long as we view the natural world and our own lives only from the perspective of work, we perceive only the functional aspect of nature and the practical features of our own bodies. When we celebrate the Sabbath, we gain the wisdom to understand the world as God's holy creation, to experience God's delight in the world, and to know that it is "very good." Remembering the Sabbath begins to reverse the alienation of humanity from God and from the other creatures of the world and it anticipates a new creation when all the earth's creatures will again be at peace with one another.

The command to "remember" the Sabbath places it in the context of God's creation: "for in six days the Lord made heaven and earth, the sea, and all that is in them, but rested on the seventh day" (Exod 20:11). By sanctifying the Sabbath, we acknowledge that God is the Creator of all things and that all of our labor must fit into God's purposes for the world. As creatures made in God's image, we are invited to participate in God's rhythm of creative activity and sacred rest.

The Sabbath year extends the principle of cyclical rest into the life of the land. In this seventh year, the sowing and reaping of the fields, as well as the pruning and picking of vines, are prohibited (Lev 25:3–4). After six years of being worked, the land is to enjoy "a Sabbath of complete rest," protecting the land from relentless exploitation and helping restore its fertility. In the seventh year, the whole society lived at a significantly lower standard of living in order to give rest to the land and to release itself from the daily grind of working the land. All the produce of the land that grew naturally during this fallow year was free to all, including the hired workers, slaves, livestock, and wild animals (Lev 25:6–7).

The Sabbath is an urgent message from an ancient time that can provide new perspective for our culture today. As ecologists and economists try to figure out how to create a just society and a sustainable economy, the Sabbath offers a reasonable direction. It encourages us to gain control over the frenetic pace of economic expansion and technological development. It urges us to pause and reflect on spiritual and moral values, to refuse to allow expansion to outstrip ethical deliberation. It shows us that an economy disengaged from social and environmental concerns will drain human energies and deplete the earth. The ancient lessons of the seventh day and the seventh year, the principles of regular resting, reflecting, and releasing, can point our way to a more hopeful future.

Reflection and discussion

• Why is keeping the Sabbath such a critical part of honoring God's covenant?

• What is the relationship between the Sabbath day and the Sabbath year? What are the principles which they hold in common?

• What is the ecological wisdom in Israel's ancient legislation for the Sabbath? How does the Sabbath promote care and protection for all God's creatures?

• What does it mean to me to keep the Sabbath holy? How can I sanctify a day of leisure, celebration, and worship in my life?

• What would it mean for the world if people viewed their lives and those of God's creatures less from the functional perspective of work and more from the contemplative perspective of Sabbath?

Prayer

Lord of the Sabbath, you call your people to respect the created rhythm of work and leisure. Teach me how to work well and rest well, always grateful for your blessings. Show me how to delight in your creation and enjoy your Sabbath peace.

They will not hurt or destroy on all my holy mountain; for the earth will be full of the knowledge of the Lord as the waters cover the sea. Isa 11:9

A Kingdom of Justice, Harmony, and Peace

ISAIAH 11:1–9

¹*A shoot shall come out from the stump of Jesse,*
  and a branch shall grow out of his roots.
²*The spirit of the Lord shall rest on him,*
  the spirit of wisdom and understanding,
  the spirit of counsel and might,
  the spirit of knowledge and the fear of the Lord.
³*His delight shall be in the fear of the Lord.*
He shall not judge by what his eyes see,
  or decide by what his ears hear;
⁴*but with righteousness he shall judge the poor,*
  and decide with equity for the meek of the earth;
he shall strike the earth with the rod of his mouth,
  and with the breath of his lips he shall kill the wicked.
⁵*Righteousness shall be the belt around his waist,*
  and faithfulness the belt around his loins.

⁶*The wolf shall live with the lamb,*
the leopard shall lie down with the kid,
the calf and the lion and the fatling together,
and a little child shall lead them.
⁷*The cow and the bear shall graze,*
their young shall lie down together;
and the lion shall eat straw like the ox.
⁸*The nursing child shall play over the hole of the asp,*
and the weaned child shall put its hand on the adder's den.
⁹*They will not hurt or destroy*
on all my holy mountain;
for the earth will be full of the knowledge of the Lord
as the waters cover the sea.

Israel's prophets often gave hope to God's people through imaginative images depicting a renewed and perfected world. The biblical vision of God's good future describes God dwelling with his people and with all the living creatures of the earth in a renewed harmony. Images from the garden of Eden portray the future reconciliation between God and humanity and between all our creaturely kin within the world. Social justice and ecological harmony are the twin characteristics of the peace God intends to establish for creation.

For ancient Israel, celebration of the Sabbath and anticipation of the coming Messiah were the primary ways in which this hope was expressed. The Sabbath was the here-and-now symbol of the joyful harmony which God intends for creation. The coming of the Messiah was the future expectation which would bring reconciliation and peace between God and humanity and between humanity and the living creatures of the world. All creation waited in joyful hope for the coming of God's anointed one.

Isaiah's image of renewed creation begins with the fallen tree of Israel's monarchy. Out of the roots of this barren stump will arise a new shoot, a new ruler from the fallen family of David, who will bring justice and peace to the land (verse 1). This future king is endowed by God's spirit with every gift for wisdom and discernment (verse 2). He will exercise true dominion, standing on behalf of the poor and meek in a world in which they are still prey for the wicked and the unjust (verses 3–5). As the one who brings God's reign to the earth, the Messiah will demonstrate God's faithfulness and bring God's desired order to creation.

This hopeful vision of the future kingdom depicts humanity in harmony with all the creatures of the earth (verses 6–9). The images of wild and dangerous animals existing together without threat or violence express the peace that the world will know when God reigns. Isaiah envisions a planet in which everything is reversed from the destruction brought about by greed and hostility. He anticipates a deep and radical transformation of the world in which humanity—like the wolf, leopard, lion, and bear—will have no desire to injure, no hunger to devour, no need for brutal domination. This picture of the world in not a world turned upside down, but it is God's original intent for creation. It is a world turned right side up.

Reflection and discussion

• In what ways are the pursuits of social justice and ecological harmony related? Why are they both necessary for God's reign?

• The reign of the Messiah is described in the prophets as an earth-centered goal. What would the world look like under the Messiah's reign?

Prayer

Faithful God, send your spirit of wisdom and understanding upon your people so that we may know your will for the world and act with justice upon the earth. Help us work for a world in which there is no need for hostility and no hunger for violence.

The mountains and the hills before you shall burst into song,
and all the trees of the field shall clap their hands. Isa 55:12

The Mountains, Trees, and Flowers Rejoice

ISAIAH 35:1–7

¹The wilderness and the dry land shall be glad,
the desert shall rejoice and blossom;
like the crocus ²it shall blossom abundantly,
and rejoice with joy and singing.
The glory of Lebanon shall be given to it,
the majesty of Carmel and Sharon.
They shall see the glory of the Lord,
the majesty of our God.

³Strengthen the weak hands,
and make firm the feeble knees.
⁴Say to those who are of a fearful heart,
"Be strong, do not fear!
Here is your God.
He will come with vengeance,
with terrible recompense.
He will come and save you."

⁵*Then the eyes of the blind shall be opened,*
and the ears of the deaf unstopped;
⁶*then the lame shall leap like a deer,*
and the tongue of the speechless sing for joy.
For waters shall break forth in the wilderness,
and streams in the desert;
⁷*the burning sand shall become a pool,*
and the thirsty ground springs of water;
the haunt of jackals shall become a swamp,
the grass shall become reeds and rushes.

ISAIAH 55:10–13

¹⁰*For as the rain and the snow come down from heaven,*
and do not return there until they have watered the earth,
making it bring forth and sprout,
giving seed to the sower and bread to the eater,
¹¹*so shall my word be that goes out from my mouth;*
it shall not return to me empty,
but it shall accomplish that which I purpose,
and succeed in the thing for which I sent it.

¹²*For you shall go out in joy,*
and be led back in peace;
the mountains and the hills before you
shall burst into song,
and all the trees of the field shall clap their hands.
¹³*Instead of the thorn shall come up the cypress;*
instead of the brier shall come up the myrtle;
and it shall be to the Lord for a memorial,
for an everlasting sign that shall not be cut off.

Throughout the Scriptures we are presented with a world fashioned, loved, and renewed by God. The Torah, psalms, and prophets all present a vision of the world in which God is at the center and in which all things exist ultimately to praise God. Within this God-centered view of the earth, human beings are both unique in the world and also part of the community of creation. The earth is home for all kinds of creatures, not only humans. God sustains all living things with his love and enters into covenant relationship with the whole world. Through the prophet Hosea, God proclaims an earth-bound future: "I will make for you a covenant on that day with the wild animals, the birds of the air, and the creeping things of the ground; and I will abolish the bow, the sword, and war from the land" (Hos 2:18). Humans are thoroughly bound up, not only with God, but with other human beings, and with every other being on this beautiful blue-green earth.

Through stunning language, the psalms and prophets express the ability of every creature, each in its own unique way, to respond to God. The earth rejoices, the sea roars, the fields exult, and the hills sing for joy (Ps 96:11–12; 98:7–8). Isaiah presents a poetic scene in which the holy land rejoices as God's people return from exile. The desert "shall blossom abundantly and rejoice with joy and singing" (35:2). Lebanon, Carmel, and Sharon, lands known for their abundant vegetation and lush beauty, serve as examples of how the land will be transformed. This delighted response of creation is linked with human encouragement and healing: the weak and feeble are strengthened, the blind and deaf are restored, the lame leap like deer, and the mute sing for joy (35:5–6). The land becomes a place where people, animals, and all living beings can flourish. Springs and streams flow through the dry desert, creating marshland, oasis, and refreshing habitat (35:6–7).

Isaiah looks to a time in which the redemption accomplished by God will bring a renewed order to the world. In this joyful time, God's peace will prevail again as it did in the garden of Eden. God's promises will be fulfilled in the world, just as surely as the rain and snow cause seeds to germinate and the earth to sprout (55:10–11). Nature joins in the rejoicing at the triumphant revelation of God's glory: "The mountains and hills shall burst into song, and all the trees of the field shall clap their hands" (55:12). The tragedy in the garden (Gen 3:18), in which human greed brought a curse to the ground causing it to bring forth thorns and thistles, is reversed. Isaiah proclaims the earth's renewed abundance: "Instead of the thorn shall come up the cypress; instead of the briar shall come up the myrtle" (55:13). This wondrous fertility of the land is described in the same language as the rainbow in the Genesis account: it is a "memorial" and "everlasting sign," both to God and to humanity, of the promises God has made.

Isaiah proclaims that people, animals, forests, mountains, rain, snow, and all created things form a symphony of praise. In the prophet's vision, all the created beings in the world are a community of thriving, abundant life, responding to their Creator. Our companions in this community of life not only surround, support, and nourish us, they also charm, fascinate, and delight us. And yes, they even praise God with us.

Reflection and discussion

• What difference does it make when humans have a God-centered view of the earth? How does this perspective change my response?

• What does a flower bursting into bloom convey to me about the earth and its purpose?

• How do the words of Isaiah offer me hope for the world and its future?

Prayer

Glorious Lord, all the creatures of the earth give you praise as you bring redemption to the world. Teach me to rejoice in the wondrous beauty of your world and help me respond to your glory with all my creaturely companions.

Be glad and rejoice forever in what I am creating;
for I am about to create Jerusalem as a joy,
and its people as a delight. Isa 65:18

God's Promise of an Earth Renewed

ISAIAH 65:17–25

[17] *For I am about to create new heavens*
  and a new earth;
the former things shall not be remembered
  or come to mind.
[18] *But be glad and rejoice forever*
  in what I am creating;
for I am about to create Jerusalem as a joy,
  and its people as a delight.
[19] *I will rejoice in Jerusalem,*
  and delight in my people;
no more shall the sound of weeping be heard in it,
  or the cry of distress.
[20] *No more shall there be in it*
  an infant that lives but a few days,
  or an old person who does not live out a lifetime;

for one who dies at a hundred years will be considered a youth,
and one who falls short of a hundred will be considered accursed.
²¹ *They shall build houses and inhabit them;*
they shall plant vineyards and eat their fruit.
²² *They shall not build and another inhabit;*
they shall not plant and another eat;
for like the days of a tree shall the days of my people be,
and my chosen shall long enjoy the work of their hands.
²³ *They shall not labor in vain,*
or bear children for calamity;
for they shall be offspring blessed by the Lord—
and their descendants as well.
²⁴ *Before they call I will answer,*
while they are yet speaking I will hear.
²⁵ *The wolf and the lamb shall feed together,*
the lion shall eat straw like the ox;
but the serpent—its food shall be dust!
They shall not hurt or destroy
on all my holy mountain, says the Lord.

The prophets of Israel always maintained the creative balance between God's promises and human responsibility. Their understanding of human life as a covenant with God implied that God's reign was always mediated through responsible systems of justice within the land. When the people prayed to God, the prophets would admonish them to integrate into their social structures the justice and mercy they desired from God. The prophets called people to practice integrity within their society in the present while at the same time assuring them of the wondrous promises which God pledged for their future.

Isaiah's vision of the new heavens and the new earth (verse 17) fosters people's hope while at the same time eliciting practical goals and actions. Social programs formed on the basis of pragmatic reasoning are essential, but for people seeking to worship and serve the world's Creator, so are divine words of inspiration, promise, and hope. God's goal of restoring creation to its intended wholeness motivates the human will to promote reform within society.

God's new creation is not a completely different kind of existence but rather the completion of God's present creation. Life in the world to come is a thoroughly earthly reality. It is not an other-worldly life of idleness, but consists of satisfying work and the enjoyment of its rewards. People still build houses to live in them and plant vineyards to enjoy their fruit (verse 21). There will still be death in the new city of Jerusalem, but only after a long and fully-satisfying life (verse 20). There will still be childbirth, but children born into this renewed world will not be confronted with a life of anxiety and terror (verse 23). God will be with his people, anticipating their every need, in a relationship of confident trust (verse 24). In this ideal life, the creatures of the earth will exist without clashing, and even the crafty serpent, representing the human tendencies toward greed, will be subdued (verse 25). God's promise for the future is an existence based on God's original desire for creation, a life in which there will be no more hurt or destruction.

God's promise of new heavens and a new earth is not a world separated from this one. God does not trash the old world and start anew. Having brought this world of wonders into existence, bonded with it in covenant, and persistently having worked to redeem it, God does not give up on it. Rather, God promises to renovate creation and bring it to its fulfillment. This is a project to which humanity can join itself. All human efforts to establish justice for the land and restore balance to the world are not for naught; they are the works of responsible stewards called to care for the world over which we have been given dominion.

Reflection and discussion

• In what ways does Isaiah's prophecy maintain a creative balance between God's promises and human responsibility for the world?

• Why are divine promises and hope so important for people working for a better world?

• How does Isaiah indicate that the future creation is not a world separated from the present world?

• How will life be different in the renewed creation promised by God?

Prayer

Sovereign God, you are continually creating and renewing the world until your promises for the earth are fulfilled. Give me the courage to strive for justice upon the earth and the dedication to work for the renovation of your world.

Therefore the land mourns, and all who live in it languish;
together with the wild animals and the birds of the air,
even the fish of the sea are perishing. Hos 4:3

The Animals, Birds, and Fish Are Dying

JEREMIAH 4:19–28

¹⁹*My anguish, my anguish! I writhe in pain!*
Oh, the walls of my heart!
My heart is beating wildly;
I cannot keep silent;
for I hear the sound of the trumpet,
the alarm of war.
²⁰*Disaster overtakes disaster,*
the whole land is laid waste.
Suddenly my tents are destroyed,
my curtains in a moment.
²¹*How long must I see the standard,*
and hear the sound of the trumpet?
²²*"For my people are foolish,*
they do not know me;

they are stupid children,
they have no understanding.
They are skilled in doing evil,
but do not know how to do good.

[23] I looked on the earth, and lo, it was waste and void;
and to the heavens, and they had no light.
[24] I looked on the mountains, and lo, they were quaking,
and all the hills moved to and fro.
[25] I looked, and lo, there was no one at all,
and all the birds of the air had fled.
[26] I looked, and lo, the fruitful land was a desert,
and all its cities were laid in ruins
before the Lord, before his fierce anger.
[27] For thus says the Lord: The whole land shall be a desolation;
yet I will not make a full end.
[28] Because of this the earth shall mourn,
and the heavens above grow black;
for I have spoken, I have purposed;
I have not relented nor will I turn back.

HOSEA 4:1–3

[1] Hear the word of the Lord, O people of Israel;
for the Lord has an indictment against the inhabitants of the land.
There is no faithfulness or loyalty,
and no knowledge of God in the land.
[2] Swearing, lying, and murder,
and stealing and adultery break out;
bloodshed follows bloodshed.
[3] Therefore the land mourns,
and all who live in it languish;
together with the wild animals
and the birds of the air,
even the fish of the sea are perishing.

Though the prophets never failed to offer God's promise and hope for the earth, they also did not hesitate to condemn God's people for defiling creation with their injustice and destructive greed. The failure of God's people to obey God's laws not only led to their captivity and exile, but caused the entire land to plunge toward destruction. Sin is humanity's refusal to live in right relationship with creation and to assume appropriate responsibility for the earth. Violating the natural laws followed by the rest of creation, the people of God devastated the creation God had given them.

Jeremiah describes this environmental destruction as the undoing of creation. The prophet's description of the earth and the heavens uses the terminology of the creation account in Genesis, yet the elements of creation return to the chaos from which they were created: "I looked on the earth, and lo, it was waste and void; and to the heavens, and they had no light" (Jer 4:23; see Gen 1:1–3). The earth returns to a formless void and the heavens revert back to darkness. Even the mountains, those solid pillars holding up the earth, are shaking (Jer 4:24). The heavens and the earth have been emptied of living creatures, and the last of the birds has flown across the horizon (Jer 4:25). The fruitful garden has been turned into a wasteland and the civilizing work of man and woman is laid in ruin (Jer 4:26). Instead of the peaceful Sabbath rest after creation, the world is left with God's "fierce anger." The joyful, divine work of creation has become desolation as a result of human sin. The Creator who loved the heavens and the earth into existence has been betrayed by the only creature made in the divine image. Human dominion has resulted in dominating destruction.

Hosea describes a world in which humanity has perverted its stewardship. Because there is "no faithfulness or loyalty, and no knowledge of God in the land" (Hos 4:1), "the land mourns" (Hos 4:3). Human sin against the law of God cuts off the springs of life from the land and threatens all areas of creation. As a consequence, the wild animals, the birds of the air, and even the fish are getting weak and dying. The ecological calamity which Hosea describes is not unlike the crisis which our environment faces today and the cause is the same. Human selfishness, arrogance, and disrespect create destruction and chaos upon the earth and destroy the natural harmony among God, human stewards, and the creatures of the earth. Such abuse is an unjust denial of God's created bounty to the birds of the sky, the animals of the earth, and the fish of the sea.

Reflection and discussion

• How do the prophets connect the effects of human sin and the defilement of creation?

• According to Hosea, how can lack of knowledge of God lead to the death of living creatures on the earth?

• What are the parallels between the poetic descriptions of these prophets and the state of the world today?

Prayer

Lord of Creation, you are in anguish as you see injustice in the land and your fierce anger rages at the destruction of what you love. Give me a passionate love for the world you have created and teach me compassion for the creatures of your world.

Let the earth bless the Lord; let it sing praise to him
and highly exalt him for ever. Dan 3:74

All Creation Sings Praise to God

DANIEL 3:57–82

57 "Bless the Lord, all you works of the Lord;
   sing praise to him and highly exalt him for ever.
58 Bless the Lord, you heavens;
   sing praise to him and highly exalt him for ever.
59 Bless the Lord, you angels of the Lord;
   sing praise to him and highly exalt him for ever.
60 Bless the Lord, all you waters above the heavens;
   sing praise to him and highly exalt him for ever.
61 Bless the Lord, all you powers of the Lord;
   sing praise to him and highly exalt him for ever.
62 Bless the Lord, sun and moon;
   sing praise to him and highly exalt him for ever.
63 Bless the Lord, stars of heaven;
   sing praise to him and highly exalt him for ever.

64 "Bless the Lord, all rain and dew;
   sing praise to him and highly exalt him for ever.

⁶⁵*Bless the Lord, all you winds;*
  sing praise to him and highly exalt him for ever.
⁶⁶*Bless the Lord, fire and heat;*
  sing praise to him and highly exalt him for ever.
⁶⁷*Bless the Lord, winter cold and summer heat;*
  sing praise to him and highly exalt him for ever.
⁶⁸*Bless the Lord, dews and falling snow;*
  sing praise to him and highly exalt him for ever.
⁶⁹*Bless the Lord, nights and days;*
  sing praise to him and highly exalt him for ever.
⁷⁰*Bless the Lord, light and darkness;*
  sing praise to him and highly exalt him for ever.
⁷¹*Bless the Lord, ice and cold;*
  sing praise to him and highly exalt him for ever.
⁷²*Bless the Lord, frosts and snows;*
  sing praise to him and highly exalt him for ever.
⁷³*Bless the Lord, lightnings and clouds;*
  sing praise to him and highly exalt him for ever.

⁷⁴*"Let the earth bless the Lord;*
  let it sing praise to him and highly exalt him for ever.
⁷⁵*Bless the Lord, mountains and hills;*
  sing praise to him and highly exalt him for ever.
⁷⁶*Bless the Lord, all that grows in the ground;*
  sing praise to him and highly exalt him for ever.
⁷⁷*Bless the Lord, seas and rivers;*
  sing praise to him and highly exalt him for ever.
⁷⁸*Bless the Lord, you springs;*
  sing praise to him and highly exalt him for ever.
⁷⁹*Bless the Lord, you whales and all that swim in the waters;*
  sing praise to him and highly exalt him for ever.
⁸⁰*Bless the Lord, all birds of the air;*
  sing praise to him and highly exalt him for ever.
⁸¹*Bless the Lord, all wild animals and cattle;*
  sing praise to him and highly exalt him for ever.
⁸²*Bless the Lord, all people on earth;*
  sing praise to him and highly exalt him for ever.

This liturgical hymn is inserted into Daniel's account of the three youths who were plunged into a burning furnace because they refused to betray their Israelite faith by worshiping a golden statue in Babylon. When they were about to suffer martyrdom, God's angel went into the flames with the youths "and made the inside of the furnace as though a moist wind were whistling through it" (verse 50). The pain of the trial disappeared in the face of the youths' trusting praise and expectant hope. This song of creation is presented as the thanksgiving raised by the three Israelite youths.

The hymn is marked by the repeated invocation, "Bless the Lord." In the Bible, blessings work in two directions: God blesses creation with his presence, graces, and goodness; in return, creation lifts up blessings to God. After receiving so many blessings from the divine generosity, the world blesses God by praising, thanking, and exalting him. The hymn is sung in antiphonal style. We can imagine the soloist or choir intoning the incantation, "Bless the Lord, all you works of the Lord" (verse 57), followed by invitations to all the elements of creation. The congregation of the faithful continuously responds with the chant, "Sing praise to him and highly exalt him for ever," giving voice to the praise and thanks of all creation.

This liturgical hymn expresses a kind of cosmic procession, beginning with the heavens populated by angels, where the sun, moon, and stars also shine. From there, the waters that are above the skies pour down in praise upon the earth in the form of rain and dew (verses 58–64). Then the winds and clouds blow, lightning flashes, and the seasons manifest their gifts with the heat of summer and the frost, ice, and snow of winter (verses 65–73).

In turn, the earth displays its beauty, beginning with the mountaintops which seem to join earth and heaven (verses 74–75). United in praise to God are the vegetation that grows on the earth and the springs, rivers, and seas with their life-giving waters. The vast animal species that live in the sea, in the sky, and on the earth offer their praise to God (verses 76–81), and finally all the people of the earth join together in creation's concert of praise (verse 82).

Giving glory to God is the ultimate purpose of creation. All human actions that diminish the beauty of the world and lessen the natural ability of its creatures to magnify the Lord diminish the praise of God upon the earth. The glory of God is creation fully alive and responsive to its Creator.

Reflection and discussion

• What natural phenomena in the sky, sea, or land help me sing praise to God?

• What attitudes within myself sometimes diminish my natural desire to give glory and thanks to God?

• How does this hymn convince me that the ultimate purpose of creation is to give glory to God?

Prayer

Worthy are you, O Lord God of all creation, to be worshiped, extolled, and glorified forever. All your creatures praise you from the earth, sea, and sky with their beauty and wonder. I want to lift up a symphony of thanks to give you honor and glory throughout the earth.

SUGGESTIONS FOR FACILITATORS, GROUP SESSION 5

1. Welcome group members and ask if anyone has any questions, announcements, or requests.

2. You may want to pray this prayer as a group:

Sovereign and Faithful Lord, the laws of Israel and the teachings of the prophets foster a world in which humanity and the creatures of the earth can live in harmony and peace. Teach us to respect your laws of Sabbath rest so that we will cultivate a space for enjoyment and delight in your creation. Show us how to work toward a world that reflects the reconciliation which you desire for the creatures of the earth. Grant us the compassion and dedication to work toward the renewal of the world you have given us.

3. Ask one or both of the following questions:
   • What most intrigued you from this week's study?
   • What makes you want to know and understand more of God's word?

4. Discuss lessons 19 through 24. Choose one or more of the questions for reflection and discussion from each lesson to talk over as a group.

5. Ask the group members to name one thing they have most appreciated about the way the group has worked during this Bible study. Ask group members to discuss any changes they might suggest in the way the group works in future studies.

6. Invite group members to complete lessons 25 through 30 on their own during the six days before the next meeting. They should write out their own answers to the questions as preparation for next week's session.

7. Discuss examples of how this study might influence and motivate you to practice works of care and compassion for the living creatures of the earth.

8. Conclude by praying aloud together the prayer at the end of one of the lessons discussed. You may want to conclude the prayer by asking members to voice prayers of thanksgiving.

Look at the birds of the air; they neither sow nor reap
nor gather into barns, and yet your heavenly Father feeds them.
Are you not of more value than they? And can any of you
by worrying add a single hour to your span of life? Matt 6:26–27

Consider the Birds of the Air and the Lilies of the Field

MATTHEW 6:24–33 ²⁴"*No one can serve two masters; for a slave will either hate the one and love the other, or be devoted to the one and despise the other. You cannot serve God and wealth.*

²⁵"*Therefore I tell you, do not worry about your life, what you will eat or what you will drink, or about your body, what you will wear. Is not life more than food, and the body more than clothing?* ²⁶*Look at the birds of the air; they neither sow nor reap nor gather into barns, and yet your heavenly Father feeds them. Are you not of more value than they?* ²⁷*And can any of you by worrying add a single hour to your span of life?* ²⁸*And why do you worry about clothing? Consider the lilies of the field, how they grow; they neither toil nor spin,* ²⁹*yet I tell you, even Solomon in all his glory was not clothed like one of these.* ³⁰*But if God so clothes the grass of the field, which is alive today and tomorrow is thrown into the oven, will he not much more clothe you—you of little faith?* ³¹*Therefore do not worry, saying, 'What will we eat?' or 'What will we drink?' or 'What will we wear?'* ³²*For*

it is the Gentiles who strive for all these things; and indeed your heavenly Father knows that you need all these things. [33] But strive first for the kingdom of God and his righteousness, and all these things will be given to you as well."

The ancient wisdom of Jesus teaches simplicity of life to his followers, a way of living that does not revolve around the quest for more wealth and possessions. He says that those who follow him must make a basic choice between serving God and serving their grasping desires for more affluence. Jesus says simply, "You cannot serve God and wealth" (verse 24).

We can distinguish whom or what we serve by looking at who or what sets our priorities and determines our daily choices. Our culture's preoccupation with material productivity and acquiring goods are symptoms of a spiritual emptiness. As long as we continue measuring our well-being by how well-off we are, we will remain unsatisfied. The teachings of Jesus on simplicity challenge us as individuals and as a culture to realize that more is not necessarily better and that wealth and genuine well-being are not correlated.

Jesus presents the "birds of the air" and the "lilies of the field" as examples of trust in God's care (verses 26–29). They direct our reflection toward the marvelous interdependence of earth's creatures, and they invite us to examine the relationships that link our human lives with other living things. When we appreciate how the balance of nature reflects the divine care for creation, we can reevaluate our frenzy to acquire so much more than our basic needs require.

Jesus urges his followers to strive first for God's kingdom and God's righteousness (verse 33). In other words, he teaches us to assess the value of all things in relation to the priorities of the world's Creator and the needs of the world's creatures. When we seek first the reign of God and his justice in the world, rather than being absorbed in our own self-interest, we become a part of a project far bigger than ourselves and far more worthy of our preoccupation. This is the conversion required for discipleship, for the service of God and not of wealth.

Today the birds of the air and the lilies of the field are threatened by environmental pollution, deforestation, and toxic pesticides. God's care for his creatures is hampered by the restless acquisitiveness that characterizes our society. Considering the birds and the lilies can convince us of the need to take on ecological virtues like simplicity of lifestyle, self-restraint in accumulating, respect for the earth, and humility before God's magnificent creation. Given the God we serve, unbridled consumerism is not worthy of our allegiance. Living in our world in a way that reflects the glory of its Creator offers far greater joy and genuine satisfaction.

Reflection and discussion

• How might our culture's obsession with material wealth and accumulating possessions be a symptom of spiritual sickness? Why are we so afraid to face the diagnosis?

• What does observing the birds and the lilies teach me about my relationship with God and creation?

• In what way is an earth-friendly way of life the source of more authentic happiness than anxious acquisitiveness?

Prayer

Divine Teacher, you direct the gaze of your disciples to the lessons offered by earth's living creatures. Show me how to live my life in a way that respects the worth and dignity of my fellow creatures of the earth. Help me set the priorities of my life in a way that will bring me genuine happiness.

The creation itself will be set free from its bondage to decay
and will obtain the freedom of the glory of the children of God.
We know that the whole creation has been groaning
in labor pains until now. Rom 8:21–22

Creation's New Birth to Freedom

ROMANS 8:18–30 [18]*I consider that the sufferings of this present time are not worth comparing with the glory about to be revealed to us.* [19]*For the creation waits with eager longing for the revealing of the children of God;* [20]*for the creation was subjected to futility, not of its own will but by the will of the one who subjected it, in hope* [21]*that the creation itself will be set free from its bondage to decay and will obtain the freedom of the glory of the children of God.* [22]*We know that the whole creation has been groaning in labor pains until now;* [23]*and not only the creation, but we ourselves, who have the first fruits of the Spirit, groan inwardly while we wait for adoption, the redemption of our bodies.* [24]*For in hope we were saved. Now hope that is seen is not hope. For who hopes for what is seen?* [25]*But if we hope for what we do not see, we wait for it with patience.*

[26]*Likewise the Spirit helps us in our weakness; for we do not know how to pray as we ought, but that very Spirit intercedes with sighs too deep for words.* [27]*And God, who searches the heart, knows what is the mind of the Spirit, because the Spirit intercedes for the saints according to the will of God.*

²⁸ *We know that all things work together for good for those who love God, who are* *called according to his purpose.* ²⁹ *For those whom he foreknew he also predestined* *to be conformed to the image of his Son, in order that he might be the firstborn* *within a large family.* ³⁰ *And those whom he predestined he also called; and those* *whom he called he also justified; and those whom he justified he also glorified.*

God's salvation of the world is too often understood exclusively in refer-ence to human beings. God's plan for creation is cosmic redemption, the renewal of the heavens and the earth, not a separation of humanity from the world. The biblical tradition demonstrates not only the links between human sin and the devastation of creation, but also the connections between redemption from sin and the restoration of creation. God's ultimate desire is the restoration and perfection of all created things in peace and tranquility.

When Paul speaks about the glory that will be revealed to us (verse 18), he tells of the splendor that creation will share with redeemed humanity. Presently material creation, along with humanity, experiences bondage and is eager for freedom. Paul says that creation is "subjected to futility" and in "bondage to decay" (verses 20–21). Life on earth is presently incapable of being what it is truly made to be; it is unable to achieve the purpose for which it was created. Yet, in every creature, human and nonhuman, God has implanted the seed of hope. All created life has a built-in urge for future glory, for a final com-pleteness and fulfillment. The material universe is bonded with humanity, both in the fall from grace and in the hope of glory. The natural world longs for the same freedom as humanity; it yearns for liberation from futility, for freedom from decay, for wholeness and purpose. This is the hope that Paul expresses: "The creation itself will be set free from its bondage to decay and will obtain the freedom of the glory of the children of God" (verse 21). It is this freedom of creation that will finally reveal the fullness of God's glory.

While yearning for redemption, "the whole creation has been groaning" (verse 22). It is not difficult to see the groaning of the natural world today, suf-fering under the effects of environmental degradation. Many of our fellow creatures are gasping under the tightening clutches of ecological injustice. Terrestrial and aquatic ecosystems, in which the many parts of the natural world are linked together for vitality, are today interlinked in pain and grief at the abuse and destruction creation is suffering.

Though the present is a time of distress for both humanity and creation, their sufferings are infused with hope. They are labor pains, pushing to give birth to the new heavens and the new earth. The entire creation will be the arena for God's final redemptive work. God will restore his violated creation to its original goodness, but this promise of the future remains for now a "hope for what we do not see" (verse 25). This hope is far more than wishful thinking, far more than our natural optimism that surely things will be better in the future. We have a sure and confident hope in God's plan for the future because we have been given a foretaste of that future through God's Spirit. The same divine Spirit that swept over the chaos at the world's creation now helps us in our weakness and intercedes to accomplish God's will among us (verses 26–27). In God's Spirit we know that God has taken control of our future and has set the destiny of creation. God will achieve a final good for those who love him and have been called according to his plan (verse 28).

Christian hope is not some sort of "pie in the sky" for which we sit back and wait. If God desires a restored harmony within creation, then that must be our aspiration, too. In hope we must cooperate with God's grace as stewards of the earth. Our certain hope enables us to work with courage and confidence in God's world. In the Spirit's presence, we can again become partners with God, joyfully working to care for God's earth, while already feeling the refreshing dew of God's healing love upon the earth.

Reflection and discussion

• How do Paul's encouraging words revise my understanding of God's plan for the future?

• What indications do I see in myself that I am meant for future glory? What indicates that the natural world is also designed to share in God's glory?

• Which words of Paul offer me the most hope for the future?

• What do I see happening in the world which gives me hope? What motivates me to anticipate God's vision for the world?

Prayer

Creator and Redeemer of the world, you desire to liberate all creation from the bondage of sin, corruption, and futility. Send your Spirit to give us confidence and courage as we work with certain hope for a better future.

Not all flesh is alike, but there is one flesh for human beings, another for animals, another for birds, and another for fish. 1 Cor 15:39

Christ's Resurrection Offers Hope for the Cosmos

1 CORINTHIANS 15:35–44 *35But someone will ask, "How are the dead raised? With what kind of body do they come?" 36Fool! What you sow does not come to life unless it dies. 37And as for what you sow, you do not sow the body that is to be, but a bare seed, perhaps of wheat or of some other grain. 38But God gives it a body as he has chosen, and to each kind of seed its own body. 39Not all flesh is alike, but there is one flesh for human beings, another for animals, another for birds, and another for fish. 40There are both heavenly bodies and earthly bodies, but the glory of the heavenly is one thing, and that of the earthly is another. 41There is one glory of the sun, and another glory of the moon, and another glory of the stars; indeed, star differs from star in glory. 42So it is with the resurrection of the dead. What is sown is perishable, what is raised is imperishable. 43It is sown in dishonor, it is raised in glory. It is sown in weakness, it is raised in power. 44It is sown a physical body, it is raised a spiritual body. If there is a physical body, there is also a spiritual body.*

The heart of Christianity and the beginning of the new creation is the bodily resurrection of Jesus Christ. No longer is the glorious new existence promised by God just a distant hope foretold by the prophets and sages of Israel. It is the wondrous new reality that God has brought into the world by raising Jesus from the dead. The risen body of Jesus is both the climax of creation and the beginning of the new creation. Our hope for the future is based on the God who raised Jesus from the dead and who shows us the meaning of our future resurrected life.

Christians often think about our future resurrection as a kind of spiritual immortality apart from the created world. But our destiny is not an individualistic deliverance from this world. As bodily creatures we are deeply embedded with the rest of creation, and our future is bound up with that of the world. Paul's vision of resurrection is cosmic, a new creation of the heavens and the earth. Our bodily resurrection will be our participation in God's new creation of all reality.

Many in the Corinthian community to whom Paul wrote believed only in continuing life after death through the survival of the soul alone, but not through a future act of new creation. This dualistic understanding of the human person—an immortal soul imprisoned within a body that dies forever—was the Greek view that dominated most of the ancient world. In response to their question, "How are the dead raised? With what kind of body do they come?" (verse 35), Paul insists that the whole human person, created by God, will be given a new, transformed bodily life through the resurrection of the dead. In answering the Corinthians, Paul uses the image of a plant springing forth from a seed (verses 36–38). The seed sown in the ground first dies, then it grows into a mature plant. No one can predict the form of the plant from the appearance of the seed because God determines what sort of body to give it. With this analogy Paul demonstrates both the radical transformation of the human body in its resurrected state and its organic continuity with the mortal body that preceded it.

Since our glorified state is indeed an embodied existence, Paul demonstrates that there are many different kinds of bodies in God's creation (verses 39–41). Each has its own distinct form, from the variety of animal life to the diverse heavenly bodies in the sky. Each member of creation has its own individual glory, and all will participate in the cosmic new creation because Christ is victorious over death. Along with all of God's splendid creation, our glorified bodies will be transformed into a new type of existence. The body in this present life is perishable and weak; the body of those risen from the dead will be imperishable and glorious.

Though the "how" of resurrection still remains a mystery, we know that God's plan for the end is not to destroy our bodies but to transform them, not to reject his creation but to redeem it. In the resurrection of Jesus the future age has already burst into the present age, so that we live now with a mixture of fulfillment and expectation. The time of reconciliation, restoration, and victory over sin and death, promised by God through the prophets, has already come upon the earth. Because of the resurrection God has renewed the world and planted the seed of the new creation. For this reason, Paul concludes his discussion of resurrection with these encouraging words: "Therefore, my beloved, be steadfast, immovable, always excelling in the work of the Lord, because you know that in the Lord your labor is not in vain" (15:58). We can do the work of the Lord on earth with confidence, knowing that in him everything we do has ultimate meaning and purpose. No work for the good of creation is ever done in vain.

Reflection and discussion

• How does the bodily resurrection of Jesus help me appreciate the eternal value of the material creation?

• What would I like to understand better about creation's future? Why hasn't God explained it better to us?

• How is Paul's teaching about resurrected life different from the Greek view that was most common in the ancient world?

• How is the bodily resurrection of Jesus the climax of God's creation as well as the assurance of creation's future?

• How does the resurrection give me confidence in doing God's work for the good of creation? What convinces me that the work I do in the Lord is never "in vain"?

Prayer

God of freedom and life, by raising Jesus from the dead you have given us the first fruit of the new creation. Thank you for destroying the power of futility and death and giving me confidence and hope in the future. Help me spend my life laboring for the good of your creation.

All things have been created through him and for him.
He himself is before all things, and in him
all things hold together. Col 1:16–17

Christ, the Firstborn of All Creation

COLOSSIANS 1:15–20 [15]*He is the image of the invisible God, the firstborn of all creation;* [16]*for in him all things in heaven and on earth were created, things visible and invisible, whether thrones or dominions or rulers or powers—all things have been created through him and for him.* [17]*He himself is before all things, and in him all things hold together.* [18]*He is the head of the body, the church; he is the beginning, the firstborn from the dead, so that he might come to have first place in everything.* [19]*For in him all the fullness of God was pleased to dwell,* [20]*and through him God was pleased to reconcile to himself all things, whether on earth or in heaven, by making peace through the blood of his cross.*

The saving love that God has manifested to the world in Jesus Christ is far broader and more encompassing than we can imagine. Paul's words about Christ shatter all of our narrow understandings of God's plan, exploding any idea we may have that salvation is just for the individual or even exclusively for the church. God's purpose is for the restoration and healing of the whole world. Paul underlines this all-inclusive vision with his steady repetition of "all things," an expression that includes every element of the created world.

This section of Paul's letter was probably part of an early Christian hymn, sung either at the baptismal or eucharistic liturgy. Those Christians knew that in baptism they were recreated through entering into the dying and rising of Christ. In each eucharistic celebration, they reentered into this saving mystery. So, as people through the ages experience God's saving power in worship and are transformed in Christ, they are sent forth with the mandate to live transformed lives. As people renewed in Christ we too go out from the assembly to restore harmony in our own lives, to seek justice within the world, and to care for all creation in a way that reflects the loving purposes of the one who has created all things. Singing this hymn will not allow the mission of discipleship to be narrowly defined.

Christ is "the image of the invisible God" (verse 15), the one in whom the nature of God has been perfectly revealed. He is, furthermore, "the firstborn of all creation," because through him and for him the entire cosmos came into being (verse 16). All supernatural powers as well as earthly rulers are subordinate to him. Not only is Christ "before all things," but "all things hold together" in him (verse 17). He is the sustaining and unifying principle of life for the world because in him "the fullness of God" dwells (verse 19).

As the complete revelation of God, Jesus Christ is the agent of both the world's creation and the world's redemption. He is both the origin and the goal of God's plan for the world. Through his saving death and resurrection, "God was pleased to reconcile to himself all things" (verse 20). This divine act of cosmic reconciliation is designed to restore the harmony of God's original creation, to bring "all things" into renewed unity and wholeness. Nothing lies outside the creative and redemptive embrace of God's grace.

The redemption and restoration of "all things" has been inaugurated in the saving actions of Christ, but clearly full tranquility among the created beings of the earth is far from complete. Through the cosmic reign of Christ we have assurance that God's purposes for creation will be fulfilled, but we also have a mandate as disciples to work as stewards of the earth to cooperate with God's grace. As people reconciled to God in Christ, we have a special responsibility to bring divine healing and restoration to all God's creatures.

Reflection and discussion

• In what way have I limited my understanding of the scope of God's saving purpose in Christ?

• How does this hymn demonstrate that divine Wisdom (Prov 8:22–31) has been fully embodied in the person of Jesus Christ?

• How does the transformation I experience in worship empower me and send me out filled with God's purpose for the world?

Prayer

God of Life, you have reconciled all things in heaven and on earth through the death and resurrection of Christ. As the firstborn from the dead, the risen Christ has assured all creation of your ultimate purpose. Help me be an instrument of healing and renewal for your whole creation.

The one who was seated on the throne said, "See, I am making all things new." Also he said, "Write this, for these words are trustworthy and true." Rev 20:5

An End to Mourning, Pain, and Death

REVELATION 21:1–27 ¹*Then I saw a new heaven and a new earth; for the first heaven and the first earth had passed away, and the sea was no more.* ²*And I saw the holy city, the new Jerusalem, coming down out of heaven from God, prepared as a bride adorned for her husband.* ³*And I heard a loud voice from the throne saying,*

"See, the home of God is among mortals.
He will dwell with them as their God;
they will be his peoples,
and God himself will be with them;
⁴*he will wipe every tear from their eyes.*
Death will be no more;
mourning and crying and pain will be no more,
for the first things have passed away."

⁵*And the one who was seated on the throne said, "See, I am making all things new." Also he said, "Write this, for these words are trustworthy and true."* ⁶*Then he said to me, "It is done! I am the Alpha and the Omega, the beginning and the end. To the thirsty I will give water as a gift from the spring of the water of life.*

[7] *Those who conquer will inherit these things, and I will be their God and they will be my children.* [8] *But as for the cowardly, the faithless, the polluted, the murderers, the fornicators, the sorcerers, the idolaters, and all liars, their place will be in the lake that burns with fire and sulfur, which is the second death."*

[9] *Then one of the seven angels who had the seven bowls full of the seven last plagues came and said to me, "Come, I will show you the bride, the wife of the Lamb."* [10] *And in the spirit he carried me away to a great, high mountain and showed me the holy city Jerusalem coming down out of heaven from God.* [11] *It has the glory of God and a radiance like a very rare jewel, like jasper, clear as crystal.* [12] *It has a great, high wall with twelve gates, and at the gates twelve angels, and on the gates are inscribed the names of the twelve tribes of the Israelites;* [13] *on the east three gates, on the north three gates, on the south three gates, and on the west three gates.* [14] *And the wall of the city has twelve foundations, and on them are the twelve names of the twelve apostles of the Lamb.*

[15] *The angel who talked to me had a measuring rod of gold to measure the city and its gates and walls.* [16] *The city lies foursquare, its length the same as its width; and he measured the city with his rod, fifteen hundred miles; its length and width and height are equal.* [17] *He also measured its wall, one hundred forty-four cubits by human measurement, which the angel was using.* [18] *The wall is built of jasper, while the city is pure gold, clear as glass.* [19] *The foundations of the wall of the city are adorned with every jewel; the first was jasper, the second sapphire, the third agate, the fourth emerald,* [20] *the fifth onyx, the sixth carnelian, the seventh chrysolite, the eighth beryl, the ninth topaz, the tenth chrysoprase, the eleventh jacinth, the twelfth amethyst.* [21] *And the twelve gates are twelve pearls, each of the gates is a single pearl, and the street of the city is pure gold, transparent as glass.*

[22] *I saw no temple in the city, for its temple is the Lord God the Almighty and the Lamb.* [23] *And the city has no need of sun or moon to shine on it, for the glory of God is its light, and its lamp is the Lamb.* [24] *The nations will walk by its light, and the kings of the earth will bring their glory into it.* [25] *Its gates will never be shut by day—and there will be no night there.* [26] *People will bring into it the glory and the honor of the nations.* [27] *But nothing unclean will enter it, nor anyone who practices abomination or falsehood, but only those who are written in the Lamb's book of life.*

The final chapters of the Bible's last book present us with a vision of the world made right and good and whole. This highly symbolic revelation, given to the visionary by the risen Christ, offers us insights into the nature of God's will for creation. This stunning text proclaims an end to the world desecrated by corruption and greed and the beginning of "a new heaven and a new earth" (verse 1). This newly created world, first prophesied by Isaiah (Isa 65:17), does not come about by the destruction of God's earthly creation. It is, rather, a completion and perfection of God's purposes for the world. Having brought this wondrous world into existence (Gen 1), established an eternal covenant with it (Gen 9), and persistently having worked to redeem it, God does not abandon the created world and start over. God instead restores the old, liberates it from bondage, and brings it to its fullness.

The risen Christ is the world's first experience of this transformed creation; he is the beginning of the new creation. As creation's firstborn, the wisdom and word of God entered fully into the created world through his sacrificial love and became the foretaste of its future glory by his resurrection from the dead. Just as there is continuity between the earthly body of Jesus and his risen body, there is continuity between the present world and the new creation. The gospel writers had the same struggles in expressing the reality of Jesus' glorified existence as the writer of Revelation had in describing the transformed world which God promises in the future.

In this renewed creation there is no longer a separation between heaven and earth. This new Jerusalem comes down out of heaven from God (verse 2). Life in this city is literally a heaven on earth. God will dwell with us and with all the creatures of the earth (verse 3). This new bond between the Creator and his creation will be like the joy, security, and intimacy of a spousal relationship. All the consequences of a corrupted world will be abolished; no more chaos, pain, death, and darkness. All the tears of grief will be wiped away (verse 4).

This vision of the renewed cosmos points us forward in hope. Even though the world today is still permeated by corruption, divided by greed, and often experiences God as far away, we are given confidence by God's assurance, "See, I am making all things new" (verse 5). God is the Alpha and the Omega; God is the Creator but also the Redeemer. The one who gave life to the world will see his plan through to its completion (verse 6). Even though our present experience of God's renewing power is often faint and fragmentary, we can find consolation and courage in this vision because we know that what we have experienced dimly will embrace us completely in the future.

The new Jerusalem symbolizes the complete fulfillment of God's plan for the world's salvation. It is a tapestry of rich biblical images expressing the fullness of God's dwelling with creation. The city itself is the perfect dimension of a cube, the ideal form, and is made of precious gold (verses 16–18). There is no temple in this new city because the city itself is the sanctuary of God's presence. No longer does God dwell in a sacred place, but is now accessible to all people and permeates all things. All the prophetic visions of creation's destiny expressed throughout the Bible have reached their full development in this wondrous bond between the Creator and his creation.

Reflection and discussion

• In what way does the risen body of Jesus give us a foretaste of the new creation? How does the risen Christ convince me that God transforms rather than destroys creation?

• How is this understanding of the world's ultimate future different from my previous outlook? How is this view more in harmony with my perception of God as the Creator?

Prayer

God of heaven and earth, the destiny of our world is to share life forever with you in an intimate bond of love. You desire to make your home among us and wipe away every tear. Help me live in joyful hope of your coming.

Let everyone who hears say, "Come." And let everyone who is thirsty come. Let anyone who wishes take the water of life as a gift. Rev 22:17

Longing for Creation's Completeness

REVELATION 22:1–21 *¹Then the angel showed me the river of the water of life, bright as crystal, flowing from the throne of God and of the Lamb ²through the middle of the street of the city. On either side of the river is the tree of life with its twelve kinds of fruit, producing its fruit each month; and the leaves of the tree are for the healing of the nations. ³Nothing accursed will be found there any more. But the throne of God and of the Lamb will be in it, and his servants will worship him; ⁴they will see his face, and his name will be on their foreheads. ⁵And there will be no more night; they need no light of lamp or sun, for the Lord God will be their light, and they will reign forever and ever.*

⁶And he said to me, "These words are trustworthy and true, for the Lord, the God of the spirits of the prophets, has sent his angel to show his servants what must soon take place."

⁷"See, I am coming soon! Blessed is the one who keeps the words of the prophecy of this book."

⁸I, John, am the one who heard and saw these things. And when I heard and saw them, I fell down to worship at the feet of the angel who showed them to me; ⁹but he said to me, "You must not do that! I am a fellow servant with you and your comrades the prophets, and with those who keep the words of this book. Worship God!"

125

[10]*And he said to me, "Do not seal up the words of the prophecy of this book, for the time is near.* [11]*Let the evildoer still do evil, and the filthy still be filthy, and the righteous still do right, and the holy still be holy."*

[12]*"See, I am coming soon; my reward is with me, to repay according to everyone's work.* [13]*I am the Alpha and the Omega, the first and the last, the beginning and the end."*

[14]*Blessed are those who wash their robes, so that they will have the right to the tree of life and may enter the city by the gates.* [15]*Outside are the dogs and sorcerers and fornicators and murderers and idolaters, and everyone who loves and practices falsehood.*

[16]*"It is I, Jesus, who sent my angel to you with this testimony for the churches. I am the root and the descendant of David, the bright morning star."*

[17]*The Spirit and the bride say, "Come."*

And let everyone who hears say, "Come."

And let everyone who is thirsty come.

Let anyone who wishes take the water of life as a gift.

[18]*I warn everyone who hears the words of the prophecy of this book: if anyone adds to them, God will add to that person the plagues described in this book;* [19]*if anyone takes away from the words of the book of this prophecy, God will take away that person's share in the tree of life and in the holy city, which are described in this book.*

[20]*The one who testifies to these things says, "Surely I am coming soon."*

Amen. Come, Lord Jesus!

[21]*The grace of the Lord Jesus be with all the saints. Amen.*

The Bible's final vision portrays God dwelling with us, at home in creation. Humanity is healed of its insatiable greed and all creatures are restored to their original wholeness. The perfected city is also a natural garden. It is Paradise restored, with a crystalline river running through it and the tree of life bearing twelve kinds of fruit year-round (verses 1–2). In the midst of this perfected creation is the throne of God and the Lamb. There we will worship God and see his face; we will be with God and in God, in such an intimate way that human language falters when trying to express its wonders (verses 3–4).

The book of Revelation is an urgent message. The visionary is told, "Do not seal up the words of the prophecy of this book" for some distant future (verse 10). The visions are not a warning that the world will end soon; rather, they are a message about how to live in the present with anticipation. Through the gift of God's Spirit, God shares with us his own longing for the fulfillment of his plans for the world. Since we already have a foretaste of God's final purposes, then God wants us to live in anticipation of its full arrival. The early Christians knew that Christ came into their midst when they prayed "Come, Lord Jesus" in their worship. We, too, celebrate the mystery of his coming, and as we worship, we receive the grace that enables us to follow him until he comes in glory (verses 21–22).

The confidence that God gives to us should shape how we live in the world. The Christian message is always a stimulant for acting on behalf of the world, never a sleeping pill lulling us to passivity. The message of the prophets ought to have an effect on how we live. The vision of a whole and perfected creation must give us inspiration, confidence, and courage to do the work of making God's vision for the world our own. In our day-to-day actions, we are called to overcome those things within the world that do not reflect the beauty and wholeness of God's purpose for creation. The way we live must be consistent with creation's ultimate destiny.

Reflection and discussion

• What is the best way to live in anticipation of God's final purpose for creation? How can both worship and social action help me work toward God's vision of the world?

• What will it be like to live in a world without pain, fear, or death, and in a cosmos that shares an intimate bond with God? What glimpses has God given me already of this new creation?

• In what way can having a dream or vision of the future inspire us to work toward a better world?

• What is the most important insight I would like to take away from this study? In what way will my life be different in the future?

Prayer

Creating and Redeeming God, you are the source of all good things and you will bring all creatures of the world to their complete wholeness. Give me inspiration through this vision to work toward a world that reflects the splendor that you desire for creation.

SUGGESTIONS FOR FACILITATORS, GROUP SESSION 6

1. Welcome group members and make any final announcements or requests.

2. You may want to pray this prayer as a group:

Creator and Redeemer of the world, through the life, death, and resurrection of Jesus you have given us confidence and hope as we look toward the future. We know that you will never abandon or give up on the world you have created and redeemed. Rather, you will restore creation to its wholeness and bring all things to their completion. Help us be instruments of healing and renewal for your creation today, and give us the vision to work toward the future you desire for the world.

3. Ask one or both of the following questions:
   • How has this study of the created world inspired you to care for the earth in a practical way?
   • In what way has this study challenged you the most?

4. Discuss lessons 25 through 30. Choose one or more of the questions for reflection and discussion from each lesson to discuss as a group.

5. Ask the group if they would like to study another in the Threshold Bible Study series. Discuss the topic and dates, and make a decision among those interested. Ask the group members to suggest people they would like to invite to participate in the next study series.

6. Ask the group to discuss the insights that stand out most from this study over the past six weeks.

7. Conclude by praying aloud the following prayer or another of your own choosing:

Holy Spirit of the living God, you inspired the writers of the Scriptures and you have guided our study during these weeks. Continue to deepen our love for the word of God in the holy Scriptures and draw us more deeply into the heart of Jesus. We thank you for the hope and inspiration you have given us, and we ask you to make us courageous in the work that lies before us. Bless us now and always with the fire of your love.

Ordering Additional Studies

Other Titles Available for Threshold Bible Study

Eucharist
Angels of God
The Feasts of Judaism
The Sacred Heart of Jesus
Jerusalem, the Holy City
The Names of Jesus
Advent Light
The Tragic and Triumphant Cross
People of the Passion
The Resurrection and the Life
Mysteries of the Rosary
The Lamb and the Beasts
Pilgrimage in the Footsteps of Jesus
The Holy Spirit and Spiritual Gifts
Stewardship of the Earth

To check availability, or for a description of each study, visit our website at www.ThresholdBibleStudy.com or call us at 1-800-321-0411.

Threshold Bible Study is available through your local bookstore or directly from the publisher. The following volume discounts are available from the publisher:

$12.95 (1–3 copies)
$11.95 (4–7 copies)
$10.95 (8–11 copies)
$9.95 (12 or more copies)